Waiting for Armageddon

A Twinoir

Michele Mansour

Maryam Mansour

Paperback ISBN: 978-1-7348831-0-7
eBook ISBN:978-1-7348831-1-4

First Edition: April 2020

Happy is the nation whose God is Jehovah

Psalms 33:12

In memory of our parents
Farris and Annie Laurie Riley Mansour,
whose love gave us the foundation we needed
to grow into the people we are today—and
look forward to becoming tomorrow.

PRELUDE

"I think you're wrong."

Oh my God, I could feel my heart constricting. What was I hearing? Never, ever, had I heard those words directed towards my mother. And yet here was my twenty-year-old college friend throwing them out carelessly, almost thoughtlessly, as we sat around our kitchen table discussing literature. I froze in anticipation of the response. Which was . . . nothing. Maybe a laugh. Are you kidding? That was it?

And wait—our mother could be wrong? It was her fearless conviction of being right that had carried our family through some turbulent times. Yet that one uncontested phrase threw everything—the whole past, and even the present—into doubt.

Up until that moment I had never questioned our journey. I knew we were in the right. I knew we had the truth on our side, and yet, and yet . . .

PROLOGUE

Ann Arbor, Michigan
September 18, 1975

Mr. Dickens
Department of Human Resources
Protective Services
14th and E Streets, N.W.
Washington, District of Columbia. 20057

Dear Sir:
re: The widow and children of Farris Mansour, deceased, of
1618 44th Street, N.W. 20007
Dear Sir:
I am the brother of Farris Mansour. What I write is part a
matter of record, part firsthand knowledge, part information
relayed to me, and part opinion.

This family is in need of immediate attention and guidance.

Farris Mansour died in the Veterans Hospital in Washington
July 24, 1974 leaving his widow, Annie Laurie and eight children.
Four; Riley, Stephen, Melanie and Peter are adults; and four;
Maryam, Michele, Paul and Matthew, are minors.

Stephen is in the U.S. Coast Guard in Hawaii. Peter recently
left home without notice or leaving an address. Riley and Melanie

and the four minors are at home. The adults are unemployed. The minors are not in school.

The eldest, Riley goes into "blind rages" and it is thought he "needs psychiatric care."

The house is bare of furniture except for desks.

The house bears a mortgage at 6%. The present value of the house is about three times the balance owed. Payments were only about $207.00 a month. Farris Mansour's Social Security, Veterans and other benefits were sufficient to make the payments and keep the family.

Annie Laurie has refused all the above benefits. She is not making the mortgage payments. She is not selling the house for its real value although even this would be tragic as she would spend the gains within a year; leaving her on the street. Even refinancing would be tragic, as the new interest would go up to about 10% and she would fritter the gain and have large payments due.

She has been selling the silver, china and furnishings. The house is sparse of furniture and food. She refuses assistance or counsel from friendly neighbors and relatives. She will not tell the name of the mortgagee (a building loan bank in Washington) to relatives who wish to save the house for her and the children. Foreclosure is impending, or possibly completed.

This conduct is more than incompetent or unwise. It is irrational; even bizarre or insane. She needs help. She possibly desires help but is waiting for it to be forced on her. She plays games, and seems to be indulging in a drama of "survival" (her own words). She cannot survive unless she is protected from herself. While she is an adult and possessed of more than average intellect, she is a child emotionally, and she is ruled by her emotions rather than her intellect. Let whomever visits her be prepared for a convincing performance of all is well.

The situation is serious enough for one person in the neighborhood to find and inform Annie Laurie's sister, and for another to find and inform her husband's sister.

Mr. Sieder, Annie Laurie's sister's husband, has expressed to me a wish to save the house and to keep and school the four youngest children.

No one wants to take away her children forcibly nor to confine her, but the children should be under competent guardianship and a committee should be appointed to protect her from her economic insanity. Will you do this if you can?

Why do we, the relatives, not take care of the situation? She won't let us. Possibly she will cooperate with an outside agency, and if she will not cooperate with you, you have the power to protect the children. And it is possibly within your bailiwick to protect her. Will you do this if you can?

I asked someone to call or go to the Recorder of Deeds, 515 D. St. NW, phone 343-0671 to secure the name of the mortgagee on the Mansour house, but the information sent me was incomplete. It gave only the book and page number recording the deed to Farris Mansour and wife. Would you call the Recorder of Deeds office and complete the necessary information as to the name of the mortgagee so we can save her the house?

I believe the children are suffering more from the home's atmosphere than for lack of material things, but would you see to it that they are in school and fed and receiving their father's due benefits—letting them know it is not charity but their due?

Thank you for your attention.

Yours truly,
Victor Mansour

CHAPTER 1

IDYLL

Neglect. Of all the things we could have complained about, that's the one thing we never felt. And yet that's why they arrested her.

Many people wonder how our family went from an upper-middle-class life in Washington, D.C. to sleeping on the streets of New York City. For us, however, it was just another step in the journey of life. At fourteen-years-old, we, the twins, were ready for an adventure—and boy, did we ever get one.

The saga began in Washington D.C. in the late 1960's, when we were about eight years old. Our mother, Annie Laurie or AL (we call her that now but growing up it was always "Mother"), loved the theater, having acted in plays wherever she lived, from Berlin, Germany to Salzburg, Austria to Charleston, South Carolina. After graduating from college she had moved to New York City from her hometown of Lexington, Kentucky to pursue an acting career. And while she often regaled us with stories of her life in the city in the early 1940's—working in a little bookshop around the corner from her Greenwich Village apartment on Gay Street, the Horn and Hardart automats, riding the subways at midnight without fear, joining John Powers Inc., a modeling and acting agency headed by John Robert Powers—she also discussed the seamier side of the theater industry, and how she hated its "casting couch mentality." So much so that it was not long before she fled New York City to a job in the English department at Stephen's College in Missouri, a position found for her by Mr. Powers. But she never lost her love for the theater and she brought that love of drama home, making every holiday, as well as days in between, magical. Not a natural homemaker (when moving to New York City, she'd wondered why her roommate felt the need to buy pots and pans), she endured the "tedium" of preparing breakfast, lunch and dinner for her eight children by making our daily life a great adventure.

Summers were endless fun, from walking the two miles to our local public swimming pool, to homemade ice-cream-sodas and popsicles, to long summer-afternoon card games of bridge, hearts, or spades. When we were toddlers, our father loved taking us twins for a walk in the baby-buggy through the neighborhood. He was fifty-two when we were born, and we got quite used to people approaching our father, saying: "Oh, how sweet! Your granddaughters?" People also always assumed our family of eight was Catholic, and for years we could never figure that one out. As we got older and could walk with our father, we would stroll the mile or so down Reservoir Road to Georgetown on a Saturday morning. He was never a fast walker, so probably did not mind the constant starts and stops: "Oh, Daddy—watch! I'm going to roll down the hill!" When we reached Wisconsin Avenue in Georgetown he'd buy *The New York Times* and visit with Doc

Galinski the druggist. Sometimes Doc would hand each of us a miniature bottle of *4711* cologne. Oh, what a treat!

Then there was reading; how we loved to immerse ourselves in a good story. We would walk to the local library—a stately, old, brick building—select our books for the next week or two, then run outside and immediately start reading under the tree on the library grounds. Sometimes it feels like we read our childhood away, but we did quite a bit of "real" living too. Nothing organized though; our mother was not fond of organized anything. She felt, it seems, that if you were destined to be great at something your talent would simply rise to the top. Perhaps this was due to her exceptional talent on the piano; as legend has it, she sat down as a four-year-old and played (with both hands!) a tune she knew, and went on to excel at the piano, no lessons needed. Also, when as a child she had begged her father—a wealthy, retired, distillery executive—for dance lessons his response had been "If you want to dance, dance." So no, nothing organized. Perhaps the fact that there was no "end-game"—no recital for music or dance, no sports play-off win— makes us feel as though we had a childhood in which we did nothing. But play we did, and we had what felt like limitless freedom in which to do it.

Foxhall Village, our neighborhood, had been developed in the 1920's and was modeled on the British town of Bath. With sidewalks, beautiful grass and tree-lined islands in the center of the streets, stunning, solid, Tudor-style row homes with alleys behind the backyards, and lots of neighborhood children, it was a wonderful place to grow up. Our home even had a wooden walkway leading from the second floor of the house to the room over the garage—right out of a Shakespearean village! Across the street was a lovely hillside, smothered in buttercups during the summer, which led down to a field and woods. And just a block away was Glover Archbold Park, where we would take long walks through the woods as our mother pointed out the jack-in-the-pulpits growing along the rock-studded creek. We spent many an endless summer day in those havens of nature, enjoying picnics, building forts, playing baseball, picking flowers . . . not to mention afternoons of sledding and snowball fights during the winters.

On summer mornings right after breakfast we'd run out of the house, gingerly closing the back-door screen so as not to rouse our father's "God dammit!" and head up the alley to knock on our best friend Marina's door. We often awakened her; she stayed up much later than we were ever allowed to. Always up to something, it was not long before we had a game-plan for the day. Since we were only allowed to watch T.V. on the week-ends—Saturday morning cartoons and Sunday night Walt Disney—we had a lot of time to be creative and come up with things to do.

One day we decided to create a neighborhood newspaper, calling it The Foxhall News. Painstakingly hand-printing each edition through several layers of carbon paper, it was an exercise in perseverance; we would start over countless times when the printing was not up to our standards. We got into a little trouble with one article complaining about a neighbor's dog getting into everyone's trash. Apparently, that was a "dining-room-table only" topic. And that may have been the final edition of the paper—we did not handle rejection well.

Another time we built a "computer," copying the idea from a story we had read. We found ourselves a big cardboard box, large enough for one of us to sit under, wrapped the entire box in tin foil, and recorded what we thought a computer sounded like (disposal grinding, banging on pots and pans). We took the whole contraption to the corner of our block and placed the box over Marina—she was a year older, and therefore had more smarts than we did—and promptly began accosting anyone who walked by, begging them to ask our computer a question. After we joined Jehovah's Witnesses (more on that to come), our oldest brother Riley decided that we could not operate the computer anymore—it involved "foretelling the future," an un-Christian activity.

Other adventures included garage sales, lemonade stands, and even inventing our own language. How we would love to know what happened to our hand-written dictionary.

As much freedom as we had, our mother was also an extraordinarily strong presence in our lives. To keep from drowning in the mundane (to her) tasks of "breakfast, lunch, and dinner" she would make the most of every outing. "Let's go on an adventure!" she would say on some quiet afternoon. Taking us four younger ones on a walk, sure enough some unplanned activity would materialize. Once we walked by railroad tracks where a train was sitting, and she started chatting with the engineer. Soon we were riding on the caboose. Our mother's imagination entered all realms. On special occasions we would get to make a wish on her "magic" ring, a large, gaudy piece of costume jewelry with a big lavender stone in the center. We would have to close our eyes, make a wish, and turn around three times. Then we would be led into her bedroom. How we loved those Kelly-green and hot-pink polka-dot sundresses we got the one time. They even had matching headscarves. Believe us, there was never a dull moment when your mother was Annie Laurie.

Our mother always encouraged creativity. She turned a third-floor bedroom into a "make-it" room, where, with plenty of construction paper, crayons, glitter, and glue we'd make Valentine's, Christmas cards, Easter baskets and more. On rainy days, she would suggest "rainy-day fun," during which we would head up to the "make-it" room for coloring, activity book entertainment, or any other new endeavor she had found for us to do.

Our older sister Melanie (number three of the eight children and seven years older than we are) taught herself to make exquisite hand-crafted crepe-paper flowers, which she would scent with perfume. Given her name by our father for her dark hair and skin, Melanie was the only one of us who really looked Lebanese—our father's heritage. She was the oldest girl, very driven, and, according to Annie Laurie, extremely competitive, especially with our mother: she always wanted to wear our mother's clothes and hats. While Annie Laurie gave her some of her clothes, we always got the feeling she was resentful of this. We did not have to guess, actually; our mother was open about how she felt about it. And Melanie was competitive with Riley too, in what seemed to be the most inconsequential things. For years, though she was right-handed, she ate with her left hand, competing with naturally left-handed Riley.

But between Melanie and us twins there was never any friction or tension. She loved spending time with us, and we always looked up to her. As a young child, surrounded by three brothers before we came along, Melanie had always wanted a playmate and perhaps with us she had found not just one, but two. (We had never experienced that longing for companionship. As twins, we always had someone to play with, confide in, walk with . . . We remember that first moment of walking alone to a job and how exposed we each felt, not only not surrounded by family, but not even having our twin sister by our side.) Melanie taught us the dance steps she was learning in her ballet class, the French she learned in school, braided our hair, walked us to school . . . On one of those walks to elementary school, we had just learned of the concept of death. Stunned, we asked Melanie, "So what's the purpose if we're all just going to die anyway?" She replied: "To have as good a time as possible, I guess."

Melanie, opinionated and strong-willed, asked us if we ever saw ourselves as the heroine in the books we read. Never happened. We just enjoyed a good story. Melanie, on the other hand, envisioned herself as Jo March in *Little Women* or Scarlet O'Hara in *Gone With the Wind.* As a big fan of Tolstoy's *War and Peace* Melanie wanted to study Russian, but it was not offered in the public schools at that time. It would never have occurred to us to want to study the language in which a book had originally been written.

She had specific ideas about how things should be and happily "marched to the beat of a different drummer." She hated how our mother tended to be such a slave to fashion: hems up, hems down, this style, now that. No, Melanie thought you should wear what worked for you, current trends be damned. She finally began designing and making many of her own clothes, unable to find what she wanted in stores.

Melanie had no friends as a teen-ager. (God, how our mother hated that word, "teen-ager." It is difficult for us to even write it). Nor, for that matter, did the rest of our older siblings have any friends that we knew of. Not only did we think you got adult names as you aged (who knew any child named Annie

Laurie or Farris?), but we also thought you did not have friends as you got older. While our parents never said "Thou shalt not have friends," (and we younger ones all had friends) or "Thou shalt not date," they did not have to. From the many conversations around the dining table we knew how our mother, if not our father, felt. You just picked up on things. When we were young, though, while this was percolating in our little minds, there was no real consciousness of it. Life was carefree and fun.

A summertime staple for our family was attending the Smithsonian Folklife Festival—the Folk Festival, we simply called it—in downtown Washington. We would all pile on the bus to get downtown, and then spend the whole day at the festival: listening in awe to a Mexican father and his eight sons on violins and guitars, strolling over to hear the melancholy sounds of the Japanese koto, watching American Indian dances, or buying a sunbonnet from a Kentucky artisan. We loved going, and our mother enjoyed the opportunity it gave us to learn something new, and the drama of it all.

Holidays were where our mother really shined, and she often told us she lived from one to the next. On a wall in our kitchen seasonal displays were ever present: turkeys and fall leaves at Thanksgiving, hearts for Valentine's Day, flags and portraits of George Washington and Abraham Lincoln for the Fourth of July, witches and black cats on Halloween. But those wall displays were the least of it.

For the Fourth of July she organized a local parade. With a string of small flags swaying across the alley behind our home, a poster of George Washington hanging on one side of the garage, and a sign announcing the parade on the other, the festivities were advertised. Neighbors began to congregate mid-afternoon, and everyone and anyone was invited to march. Tall and lanky (at five-foot six she was just an inch shorter than our father), once described as a "handsome woman," and with a commanding voice designed to put the fear of God into anyone who heard it, our mother started coordinating the event. Dressed in a navy and red color-blocked shift with her short, no-nonsense, prematurely gray (and self-cut) hair bound by a scarf to add panache, orders were forthcoming. (The scarf played a role when our parents travelled to Europe via ship. One day a rumor spread that Betty Davis was aboard. It was our mother, in headscarf. No joke, she had Betty Davis' eyes). Soon, the line-up was in place. Our father, wearing slacks, a short-sleeved button-down shirt, and wingtip shoes, ever-present cigarette in hand, commanded "Forward, march!" and off we would go. Led by a neighbor holding a large American flag, we twins followed, dressed in our own color-blocked red, white and blue dresses and carrying a banner that stretched across the alley proclaiming: *Spirit of '76*. Stephen (number two), Melanie and Peter (number four) marched behind us, all decked out as the American revolutionaries portrayed in the painting *Yankee Doodle*, later renamed *The Spirit of '76*. Neighbors and friends followed: mothers pushing strollers, children on bikes bedecked in patriotic streamers, others simply waving flags. Around the neighborhood we marched, with people flocking to their porches as the procession passed by. Afterwards all were invited to our backyard for lemonade, and in the evening we'd set off sparklers and fireworks.

Halloween was an unforgettable celebration as well. How Annie Laurie loved its haunting, howling, horridness. She would never stoop so low as to go for a Disney costume, nor any store-bought costume. Disney, as she always, emphatically, let us know, turned classic and scary Grimm's fairy tales into maudlin movies. She was the star on Halloween, a frightening witch in her hideous, wart-filled, long-nosed mask, a peaked black hat, and a gypsy outfit of some sort. We were her two black cats wearing simple black leotards and tights. As she sat on our front porch stirring a deep cast-iron pot full of candy corn, the neighborhood children approached the house timidly "trick-or-treating." She dropped one piece of candy corn into each bag, snarling "Here's a nice piece of candy for you . . . but don't eat it, it's poison— Ahahaha!" It was a fear-inducing cackle.

And Christmas, well, what could get more magical or theatrical than that? Our parents had spent the post-World War II era in Berlin, where our father's job with the Federal government had been to encourage German scientists to emigrate to the United States rather than go to Russia to work. We often heard about the many conversations our father had been a part of, in which the discussions revolved around the types of food men would be eating on the moon—seemingly science-fiction at the time. Not however, when you are in the company of Wernher von Braun. That renowned aerospace engineer was among the men with whom our father worked. But we digress . . .

Those years in Germany had instilled in our mother an even greater appreciation for the beauty of Christmas than she already had. There was the brass angel-chime which sat on the mantel and tinkled delicately as the smoke from its four miniature candles ascended and stirred the angels to chime the bells. And how we all adored the German music-box with its little perforated-tin discs, sitting alongside the angel-chime. Our mother wound it up and "Joy to the World" played as we all descended the steps on Christmas morning. No chaotic running and randomly opening presents for us. We aligned at the top of the steps like the Trapp family, then, after hearing our mother's "ok," paraded down youngest to oldest as she and our father stood by the fireplace. The presents would be handed out one at a time, each to be savored and appreciated before the next one could be opened. And save the wrapping paper!

Our mother thoughtfully made sure that, while the two of us pretty much always got similar gifts, they were not exactly alike. One year we each got a book, both beautifully illustrated editions from the same publisher, but unique to each of us: *Hans Brinker, or The Silver Skates* for one, *A Little Princess* for the other. Sometimes we were given the same gift but with different patterns—perhaps playing cards or clothes, and we would get to pick which one we wanted. One of us would always defer to the other, even though we knew which one we liked better. Of course, the other always chose the one that the deferring one would have picked. Twins! We did get identical bicycles one year—royal blue Raleighs. Oh, did we love them. Our mother must have been as excited to give them to us as we were to receive them, because she allowed us to ride them that very day, despite the mushy snow lingering in our alley. Peter, four years our senior and a constant annoyance to us, mocked our novice riding skills, ridiculing our inability to navigate the narrow alley turn without putting our foot on the ground for balance. Ugh—older brothers.

But by far the most wonderful aspect of our childhood was the theater, *our* theater. Actress that she was, Annie Laurie turned our car-less garage into a theater. Having stopped driving after we, the twins (numbers five and six) were born—"I refuse to be a chauffeur" was how she always, emphatically, explained that decision—and since our father had never learned to drive at all, the garage was available for her creative use. How those summer Friday afternoons buzzed with excitement. It was palpable, we could feel it—theater night!

We would come home from school in late spring, the afternoon sun beaming down through the budding trees, and there it would be, the music wafting up the alley. Oh, yay! The Beatles? No. Petula Clark? No. The Symones? No, not on theater night. Usually it would be an overture our mother loved, perhaps from Mozart's *The Marriage of Figaro* or Rossini's *The Barber of Seville*. Whatever it was, we knew it meant one thing: theater season was here!

Annie Laurie had a fancy, two-speaker floor-model Fischer record player that only she was allowed to handle, since of course only she would use it properly. The music blared as she and Melanie, legal pads in hand, discussed the upcoming Friday play. There was always an opening number, which we younger girls, including our friends, would get to be in. After one of us excitedly peeked through the red curtain to see how crowded the garage was—and informed the rest of us "It's packed!"—the music started, the curtain parted, and there we were, kicking high in a chorus line, dancing as the Follies Bergere, or belting out "Let Me Entertain You" from *Gypsy*, all dressed up in fancy costumes. What fun we had wearing those dresses. Our friend Marina always seemed to be struggling to keep her green strapless taffeta dress up, one hand constantly tugging at the dress as she danced and sang her heart out. The neighbors and friends so enjoyed the performances that they donated the clothes which filled our costume room in the basement.

After the opening number there would be a *tableau* or a
current event. The tableau starred a neighbor—adult or child—
who resembled a famous painting. The neighbor would hold the
pose of the portrait while wearing the appropriate clothing. Some
of the pictures that come to mind are Fragonard's *The Girl
Reading,* George Romney's *Miss Willoughby,* Paul Cezanne's
Artist's Father Reading, and Rembrandt's *Girl with a Broo*m. We
like to brag that our childhood playmate Yeardley Smith
discovered her love of drama at the Foxhall Theater, crediting it
as she did in her 2004 one-woman Off-Broadway show *More.* She
went from posing as Mary Cassatt's *Child in a Straw Hat* in one of
our Friday night shows to becoming the voice of Lisa Simpson on
the long-running and award-winning television show *The
Simpsons.*

A current event reflected a news topic of the day. One that
got big laughs was the time our father, dressed as Ari Onassis, sat
beside a neighbor playing Jackie Kennedy. He would clap his
hands, and as he did a servant appeared and presented a gift of
pearls to Jackie; he continued to clap, and more gifts would
appear until Jackie was covered in jewels. Other current-events
depicted included the moon-landing—complete with dry ice
evoking space—and State occasions involving the Middle East, in
which our neighbor "Granny," who looked just like Golda Meir,
played the Israeli Prime Minister.

Intermission occurred before the main show. This involved
our oldest brother Riley entertaining the children with a puppet
show, performed through the side window in the garage. Riley,
eleven years older than we are, was always our biggest
cheerleader, and loved entertaining us. Born in Germany and one
of twins (the other had died "in-utero," shocking the attending

doctors at the time of his birth), when we were about four or five Riley would go into a closet and emerge as "Rudolph," his missing twin brother, speaking in his attempt at a German accent. While initially we got a kick out of this, Riley did not seem to realize that as we got older this was just not funny to us anymore. In his mind we were still five years old. To this day, Riley is more comfortable around children than adults, though perhaps that is because his method of communication tends toward lecture rather than dialogue!

Though conferred with many of the privileges of an oldest son, Riley never took on the responsibilities; we always felt we had to take care of him. As we grew, we became very resentful of this. Born with thumbs that did not work properly—they had no joints—it seemed our mother always used this as an excuse for Riley not being capable of doing certain things. But he was smart as a whip and would argue any point just for the sake of argument, whether he believed it or not. Our New York cousins loved to get him riled up when they visited, saying anything to get a rise out of him. As we grew older, we just could not understand why this "handicap" was considered such a big deal. So it kept him out of the Air Force; but why even apply for a job that has physical qualifications? Why not turn your talents in another direction? But no, all we heard from our mother was that Riley was rejected by the Air Force because of his thumbs. That was Riley's first and last attempt at a career.

But back to the theater!

After the intermission it was on to the main event, usually a musical. *My Fair Lady, Gigi, Fiddler on the Roof, The Sound of Music, The Music Man*—those shows held the songs of our youth. While our New York cousins had introduced our older siblings to the Beatles and The Rolling Stones, the musicals were the soundtrack of our childhood, and we can recite the songs today, remembering every word. (Though everyone knew the lyrics, we sang along with the records for the shows.) Thanks to our mother, we were exposed to all kinds of music growing up, and not just the classics; she loved *The Fifth Dimension's* "Age of Aquarius" and often blasted that on her Fischer machine.

All the neighbors, adults and children, participated in the productions; the Foxhall Theater was *not* children's theater, as our mother emphatically (emphatic seemed to be her default mode) let us know. Several times our theater even competed in local competitions. Oh, we were so excited! To be on a "real" stage! As Annie Laurie began the casting for a production of *Ali Baba*, my heart almost exploded as she mentioned me for the role of a water girl. We were always in minor roles, usually together, so the thought of having a special role for myself in this fancy production was thrilling. Not ten minutes later, however, Annie Laurie thought of someone else for the role, our Greek friend Elena. I was devastated but did not say a word. It never occurred to me to dispute our mother's wisdom. She was very mindful of sharing the theater with the neighbors, and not wanting to put her own children ahead of others. Our mother never knew how I felt—perhaps I inherited her acting genes after all.

Annie Laurie attempted to make our garage theater as professional as possible, not just with the acting, but with the physical environment as well. We had spotlights, posters, and even a black light to keep up with the times. Many of the posters created by our brother Stephen glowed when that black light shone on their fluorescent paint. A green carpet covered the floor, with a red curtain hanging towards the rear, separating the stage from the audience. In a surreal dichotomy, a poster of Rudolph Valentino (our mother's youthful idol) from his movie *The Sheik* shared a back wall with a psychedelic poster promoting LSD— this *was* the 1960's.

Just outside the garage was the "café." We grew up hearing of the charming Parisian cafés our mother had loved when touring Europe, and since none were to be found at that time in D.C., she created her own: *un charmant cafe a l'exterieur du garage.* One or two tables, placed right outside the garage and covered in checked cloths, were surrounded by directors' chairs. Above, a cheery yellow-striped awning covered the patio, and the entire area was bordered by an oversized, custom-made flower box. She loved marigolds, geraniums, petunias, and impatiens, to such an extent that she petitioned (and won) to have our alley named "Marigold Way." Posters advertising the upcoming show hung on either side of the exterior of the garage.

On theater nights, our father was responsible for dinner. Often it was cucumbers and yogurt with mint, a meal he fondly remembered from his Lebanese upbringing (though he was born and raised in the United States, his parents were immigrants, and he spoke Arabic until he went to school at seven years old). Occasionally he would add some bologna as a side—a food he probably thought was an abomination. Sometimes he would walk around our dining room table throwing a slice onto each plate, muttering "Here, eat this *chudda.*" (that's Arabic for sh*t). But it was quick and easy for theater night and we loved it.

Fridays, however, were all about the show. We would inhale our dinner then run back to the garage to see what was going on. Could we get into our costumes yet?!! Were we allowed to wear the new headdresses Mother had just bought at

the costume shop? Oh my gosh, it was so exciting! Finally, dusk
arrived and the garage began to fill up, with all the children sitting
on the floor of the interior and all the adult neighbors standing in
the rear. Sometimes the crowd reached all the way across the
alley! Our good friend Marina was the curtain puller, a
particularly important job according to our mother—timing was
essential. "Quiet, quiet" our mother hissed as she carefully placed
the needle on the record, then ducked off-stage. The music
blared, the curtain opened with a swift *swish* and the
entertainment started.

Annie Laurie encouraged everyone to mingle after the show.
She loved the camaraderie of the theater world, and how it took
her away from the "drudgery of breakfast, lunch and dinner."
Discussions ranged from critiques of the show to politics and
religion—anything but the mundane. How she hated the
mundane. Beer, wine, and snacks were served to the adults while
all we children played in the dark alleys, trying to stay as far away
as possible from our parents so they would forget we were still
up. It was a carefree and idyllic time.

CHAPTER 2

REALITY

Our life was not simply a matter of celebrating one holiday after another, though that is probably how our mother survived the "daily drudgery," as she always condemned it, of breakfast, lunch and dinner. (Have we mentioned this before? It was a constant refrain throughout our childhood). No, we went to school, and public school it was. While most of our neighborhood friends attended private or Catholic schools, our parents were big believers in the public-school system, and all eight of us attended them.

But the public schools of 1970's D.C. were not the public schools of Kentucky in the 1930's, where our mother had grown up. The D.C. schools were, to put it kindly, a mess. Years later, our mother would say of a D.C. public education in the 1960's: "It's an experience I wouldn't wish on a dog, but I wouldn't take it away from you now that you've had it."

She always described it as a slow progression (regression?), with the high school which our oldest siblings attended being the first to disintegrate. The dress code went by the wayside, and then, in a metaphor for what was to come in the standards of the education itself, the cafeteria went from using china plates to paper plates. While there remained some excellent teachers, overall the school system was deteriorating. Experimentation with new concepts (let's have open classrooms!) basically wrought havoc on getting an education. Administrators began to exert control over the teachers, hampering their ability to teach, and some teachers were simply incompetent. When Stephen, who loved math, began to hate the subject his senior year due to an inept teacher, she knew it was the beginning of the end.

Sixteen years behind Riley was Matthew, our youngest brother. Though Annie Laurie had taught Matthew to love books by reading to him (as she had to all of us) before he entered school, he was barely literate by the fourth grade. And she was furious. She had planned so far in advance that she had decided not to teach us to read so that we would not be bored when we entered school. But she had done her job by making sure we were *ready* to learn; she had instilled in all of us a love of learning and a desire to seek out answers. And now the schools had failed to do their part.

Our brother Paul (number seven and three years younger than we are) was a prime example of how she not only readied us for school but took up the slack as the public schools began to fail. She often joked that had he been her first child he might have been her last. Today, he would likely be diagnosed with ADD and put on Ritalin. But control freak that she was (she recognized this and when we were adults bought us a book about having controlling parents and how to deal with it) she was not about to let *him* control *her.* At mealtimes, when he'd put up a fight about being put in a highchair, she would have Riley strap him into the chair so that he would sit still for the twenty minutes or so it took to get him to eat. As he got a little older, in order to "channel his energy," (her words) she would give him a deck of cards, sit him down on the floor, and have him search for the ace of spades. When he found that card she would then have him search for the ace of diamonds, and so on.

After Paul entered first grade, when she began to realize the schools were failing in their job, our mother had the insightful idea to use cooking to help him learn reading and math. He was not one to sit still for long, so she kept him busy measuring flour and salt while she pointed out the words in the recipe. For math, she would double or halve the recipe and have him figure out the new amounts. Being able to remain active while learning kept his interest up. Paul is a voracious reader today; as he often remarks, "all you have to do is read one book on a subject to know more than the so-called experts."

As for us, in elementary school we were the perfect, little, obedient students, running home to do our homework *before* we went out to play. We certainly did not have hours of homework like our friends in Catholic school did (perhaps an indication of the decline in the public education system?). But we fit in and felt at ease there. Of junior high, on the other hand, we have only a few, though painful, recollections.

We became masters at ignoring what was going on around us. On the first day of junior-high, as two undeveloped, shy, and awkward twelve-year-old girls knowing essentially no-one else in the building, we gathered our courage and mounted the steps to our new school. Many of the students were hanging out in front, talking and laughing. One, a quite well-developed black girl,

decided we needed some attention: "Where your titties at, girls?"
Looking neither right nor left, we strode inside as if we had not
heard a word.

At lunch, I would head to the back of the playground, a
concrete jungle with chain-link fencing that many of us called St.
Elizabeth's, a reference to the local insane asylum. Sitting there
by myself—I wanted to minimize the awkwardness of being *two*
out-of-place students—I would be offered a toke of pot by some
of the girls hanging around nearby. I always declined the offer
and was not even tempted. Despite feeling egregiously out-of-
place in junior high school we never turned to drugs or alcohol.
Perhaps because at home was a family where we felt very much
in place.

Another time I was sitting in a classroom in which four desks
faced each other. Apparently, I had an attitude, because one day
the black girl sitting across from me said "Don't you roll your
eyes at me." Not knowing what that expression meant, nor,
really, that I was even doing it, I promptly rolled them again. "I
said "Don't you *roll* your eyes at me!" At recess, the classmate got
her revenge, coming at me with half an orange and rubbing it in
my face. It was not until years later that I learned what "rolling
your eyes" meant.

It was also the first time I realized that some black people
often see white people just as some white people often see black
people. In a classroom of about twenty-five students, there were
three white female students—two blond-haired girls and me. Our
black teacher, before heading to the hallway for a smoke (while
leaving the students to answer some questions at the back of the
textbook) called on one of the blond girls by the wrong name. He

then muttered as he walked out the door: "All you white girls look alike." Was that an eye-opener!

A final junior-high tale: Standing at my locker when a bunch of boys came down the hall and pulled up my skirt—we were still wearing skirts when just about all the other girls wore pants. One of the group, who had been in elementary school with us, quickly blurted "Don't do that; she's a Jehovah's Witness." Show some respect, in other words. Speaking of which . . .

CHAPTER 3

TRUTH

When we were about ten came the event that could be described as—what? The beginning of the end of life as we knew it? That seems fairly accurate. Our mother always said it was a culmination of her life up to that point. Or something like that. And maybe it was. But let us assure you, when you are a child the effect of such an event on your life is a bit more profound. In 1971, the "Truth," via Jehovah's Witnesses, came knocking at our door.

Now it wasn't as if we weren't used to different religions— Annie Laurie had studied with the Mormons and Catholics, our father (of Lebanese descent though not Moslem) had taken us to a mosque, and once we even sang in the all-black choir of an AME church. And that was on top of our "regular" church-going Sundays, when we would walk the block-and-a-half to the bus stop and take the D4 downtown to National City Christian Church. Though even there we did not just show up. We would make Easter baskets for the organist and deliver them to him at the organ, where we would get to see him play up close. Or there was the time our older sister Melanie made a Valentine for President Johnson (he attended "our" church) and presented it to him at coffee hour. She wanted us to go with her, so we could meet him, but little "'fraidy cats" that we were we hung back. Her picture appeared in newspapers world-wide, handing the President a Valentine as he leaned over to accept it from her.

After church we would get to go out to eat, in the early years to a local cafeteria, and then, when the first one opened in downtown D.C., to McDonalds. Oh, what an incredible treat that was. We were in awe of the crew—all young black men—any of whom would memorize the entire family's order and then repeat it back to us. Our mother always made sure we appreciated their talent and hard work. Following that we would go to one of the many museums in downtown Washington, though our mother never let us get overwhelmed. We would head to one wing of the

National Gallery of Art and look at just a few pictures, and that
would be it for the day.

But the "Truth," well, this was different. First of all, it wasn't
just a Sunday thing, but a whole way of life thing. And it was not
a fall-on-your-knees, blinded-by-the-light, kind of truth. No, this
"Truth" involved study, study of the Bible.

After that initial knock on the door—is there anyone in
America who has not had that experience?—our mother not only
opens the door, but invites the two Witnesses in. Soon Jennie
Rose and her fourteen-year-old son become a weekly fixture at
our house. While our father remained apart, never a fan of
organized religion, our mother, along with Stephen and Melanie,
jumped wholeheartedly into the Bible study. They began going to
the Kingdom Hall on Sunday for the talks, and it was not long
before we four younger ones were brought along on this new
journey. Since we did not have a car, and the bus route didn't go
that way, we would walk the two miles to the Kingdom Hall as a
family. At ten or eleven years old, we were used to being
different, so this didn't faze us in the least. (We identified with the
children when our mother talked about how hard it must have
been for a black mother during segregation to tell her children
that they could not do certain things. As Mansours, we did not do
certain things either.) Before long we were memorizing the books
of the Bible, reciting Scriptures, and diligently studying the
Watchtower Magazine, a publication of the Witnesses edifying
their take on Biblical matters. In an ironic twist, our mother's
familiar, wistful lament "If only you knew the Bible as well as you
know those commercials!" was beginning to come true: we were
learning the Bible. Though we had never been allowed to watch
much television, and even had to cover the screen with a

dishtowel during commercials to "rest your eyes," somehow we had managed to effortlessly learn the advertising jingles.

Around this time Stephen, twenty-years-old, made a trip to visit to our cousins on Long Island, and considered a move to New York to work for our uncle, who ran a printing press in Manhattan. When Jennie Rose, the Jehovah's Witness who by now had become a family friend, heard of his plan she made the comment "I don't think it's a good idea for you to be away from your mother's influence." That clinched it; Stephen immediately stopped going to Kingdom Hall, realizing he would never grow up if he continually followed whatever his mother was doing. And while the job in New York did not pan out, Stephen knew he needed to find work. Having spent the year after high school "helping out around the house," as he described it—much to the chagrin of the Civics teacher he had run into—he decided that working for a printing company sounded interesting. Taking the bus downtown, he entered every print shop he walked by, asking to be an apprentice. The third one hired him.

When Stephen stopped his association with the Witnesses, Riley jumped in. And has never looked back.

Studying the Bible wasn't the only aspect of being a Witness. If you started to really believe (and boy, did we ever) then you had to spread the Word. And if you think adolescence is trying, try knocking on a stranger's door as a bucked-tooth, stringy-haired, glasses-wearing, socially ill-at-ease eleven-year-old, and telling the person who answers the door that you're bringing them the "Truth." Talk about painful.

And so, enveloped in the Witnesses' teachings, our life began to change, with our mother whole-heartedly adopting the Witnesses' beliefs. There was the first year we stopped celebrating Christmas, when the neighbors came peeking through the window to see if, indeed, we really did not have a tree. And we did not.

And she was so gung-ho that for our very first "vacation" we went to New York City to attend a three-day convention of Jehovah's Witnesses at Yankee Stadium. After our mother attempted to convert our Jewish hotel manager (have we mentioned she was gung-ho?) we would get on the subway and head to the stadium, where the July heat, the umbrella-hats that attendees were wearing for shade, and the hand-held electric fans—some even sprayed water!—people used to keep cool were what we as children most remembered about the convention. The crowd was a record for the stadium at 70,000 attendees, and our mother raved about the ability of the Witnesses to organize and run such a large event so efficiently. She also loved the presence of all the international guests, many wearing the colorful garb of their nations, and tried to meet and introduce us to as many of them as possible.

Following right along with the Witnesses' teachings, celebrating birthdays was now out. Whereas before the Witnesses came into our lives, "shut up" was considered a bad word in our family, now sinning was as simple as saying "Happy Birthday." Friday night plays were also eliminated, replaced with Bible study groups at Kingdom Hall.

Our mother tried to get our father interested in the Witnesses' teachings, but it never really worked. He may have gone to a meeting once. Farris was not a churchgoer, so this new "Truth" was a hard sell that he never bought. He was so far removed from religion that he used to tell us that he was born full-grown, having been "pulled from the ear of Zeus." And to our young minds this was entirely plausible, as we had an awfully hard time imagining our older, professorial father as a child! When he casually brought up a boyhood recollection during dinner one evening, I jumped up and said, "See Daddy, you *were* a boy!" He tried to back track, "Oh did I say that?" I pushed and pushed, insisting, "I heard you!" He finally with a hint of pique responded "Yes, I was a boy." And I was immediately deflated. I had liked it when he lightheartedly insisted he was never a child, and I had not really wanted him to "win" that argument.

Despite our father's antipathy to organized religion, our mother always thought that if he ever did join a religion, the Witnesses would be it; it made so much sense to her and, as she often told us in later years, she felt the Witnesses' interpretation of the Bible embodied his whole outlook on life. "Religion is a way of life," he had always said. In the end it just become a divisive factor in their marriage, as well as in the family as a whole.

At this point the Witness lifestyle was beginning to overwhelm our family, with almost all conversations now revolving around Biblical topics. As we noted, Stephen had reached the point where he just wanted to get away from it all. He and our brother Peter were trying to rebel a bit, though rebelling can be difficult when your mother encourages you to grow your hair long, as our mother encouraged Stephen, and considers herself a natural-born hippie/feminist. Peter did put a huge poster of a bikini-clad Raquel Welch on his bedroom wall. Oh, scandal! This was not "mother-approved" rebelling. And then Stephen announced he was going to join the Coast Guard. As the child of a Jehovah's Witness, that would certainly be considered rebelling. The Witnesses do not participate in "earthly governments," believing as they do that no man-made government will succeed. Only government under God will ultimately be successful.

But the Coast Guard *was* the least militaristic of the four armed services, in our mother's mind, anyway. She saw their main mission as protecting the coastline, whereas the Army, Air Force and Marines were primarily fighting operations. Stephen was ready to rebel, but only up to a point! He enlisted, and after boot-camp, when he could request where he wanted to be stationed, he asked for Hawaii, about as far away from home as he could get. He got the assignment.

On leave, Stephen returned from Hawaii a year later bearing gifts of pukka shell necklaces and kukui nut bracelets. When not in training, he had made the most of his time in Hawaii by biking all over the pineapple groves studded throughout the island. We saw quite a transformation—he had changed from our pale, nerdy, math-freak brother into a tanned and fit young man.

Our mother, however, was not one to belong to any group for long. After diving headfirst into the "Truth," and not only getting herself baptized but having Riley, Melanie and then Peter join her, she soon started having issues with the Witnesses. Annie Laurie never seemed to think that rules were meant for her.

Then came the "big split." Our mother wanted Riley to go to work at Bethel, the Witness headquarters in Brooklyn Heights, NewYork, where all the Witness publications are printed. Riley appeared to want to go, though often he seemed to just go along with whatever she wanted for him. However, there were certain requirements of the Witnesses that needed to be fulfilled before he could apply to Bethel; namely that he had to be a pioneer (knock on doors) with his local D.C. congregation for at least two years first.

Well, this was just too much for our mother. How absurd! Of *course* Riley was qualified to go to Bethel! As Riley argued with the elders: "But it might be too late by then! Don't you believe what you're preaching?! If Armageddon is coming in 1975, I don't have *time* to pioneer for two years. There are what—four billion people on earth? And how many Witnesses? Knocking on one door at a time is not the most effective way to spread the word. Do you want to condemn all those people to death?!! We've got to do something *more!"*

And now for the straw that broke the camel's back. During this meeting with the elders, one of them told Riley that he was "too short" to go to Bethel. He needed to be "big and tall like Joe Dillburger" (a member of our congregation who had just been accepted to Bethel). Out spewed our mother's venom: "Are you out of your mind? This is worse than the insanity of the public schools!" Riley proclaimed the elders "Satan's co-horts," and told them this was nothing other than a "quadruple fulfillment of Isaiah." (They had taught him well—he sure knew his Bible).

"*What?*!" The elders were stunned. "Did you mean what you just said, Riley?" He sure did. And our mother and Melanie concurred.

Kicked out! For "conduct unbecoming a Christian" all three were disfellowshipped, that is, ex-communicated. Just like that, our formal association with Jehovah's Witnesses ended. But whatever our mother did she did with conviction and drama, and getting kicked out of the "Truth" was no exception.

Over long conversations with Riley, Melanie and our father about the events that led to the disfellowshipping, our mother began to see the humor in the situation. She started pulling together lyrics for songs, composing tunes on the piano while Melanie wrote down the lines. Soon they came up with several songs and scenes. Annie Laurie intended to turn the whole story into a musical comedy called *Oh, Brother!* (Jehovah's Witnesses address each other as Brother or Sister followed by the person's last name). This was decades before the *Book of Mormon* hit Broadway! Here's a sample of one of the songs:

> Oh, brother, Oh, brother knock on the door
> Oh, brother, Oh, brother that's what we're for
> Open the Bible and we'll preach the Word
> Armageddon's coming-
> Or haven't you heard?
>
> Oh, brother, Oh, brother knock on the door
> Oh, brother, Oh, brother that's what we're for
> No other pleasure does this old world hold
> But that you join the fold!

With our mother's enthusiasm for whatever the latest pursuit, we took our changes in stride: magical Christmas, then no Christmas; birthdays, then no birthdays; church, no church; Kingdom Hall, no Kingdom Hall. We never complained or thought about whether we were happy or not. We simply lived life guided by our parents. Perhaps our mother's conviction was so strong that we followed right along without a second thought.

And then came another turning point, which shifted our lives yet again.

CHAPTER 4

GRIEF

Our father, Farris, at sixty-four, looked like a much older man. Some of that was due to the era he grew up in. Born in 1909, he always dressed formally, and rather elegantly—he enjoyed nice clothes. We never saw him in a pair of jeans, let alone a t-shirt. At times he would wear an ascot in the summer, with Bermuda shorts, knee socks and sandals completing the look. But there seemed to be a despair about him that aged him more than mere attire could have. In 1973, the only job he could get was as a substitute teacher in the D.C. school system. This, combined with a family going in a direction without him, must certainly have been demoralizing. This letter to Stephen reveals a bit of his state of mind at the time:

November 24th, 1973

Dear Stephen,

I don't know how all this happened but here we are in Manhattan once again. Tomorrow we return to Washington or at least I will.

Wednesday I came home early from school when Annie Laurie, Riley, and Melanie stunned me with the notice. They were shocked that I agreed, and the more I thought about it, the more shocked at myself I was for agreeing. Then we thought of leaving the four little ones behind with me to take care of them, but by the time we had resolved the matter it was too late for we had told them otherwise.

I expect Mother will write you more in detail and the children as well. It was a wild idea on the part of the older ones (except Peter) and I went along with it for various reasons. (One is that I may never again be able to do something for and with them.)

A.L., Riley and Melanie went to Bethel in Brooklyn, spending the day there. Peter went to the Bronx Zoo. We ate at a Greek place, on meat pies, etc.

I don't know how "successful" the trip was. I had expected to rest and to do a few chores that needed doing (I have no "workless" days until Christmas). Well, I shall try to work it out somehow.

Stephen, we enjoy your letters. We talk of you constantly and many things bring you to mind.

Love,

Daddy

We began to hear arguments spring up between our parents after we had gone to bed, with the slam of the front door signifying the fight over as our father stormed out for a smoke and to walk off his anger. (Ah—how we have perfected that form of handling disagreements! Years later, when the anti-smoking brigade broke out in full-force, our mother always wondered: Have they done any studies showing that taking a cigarette break might prevent people from doing or saying something they would later come to regret?) An excerpt from a letter written to Stephen in Hawaii makes clear our father's emotions:

April 24, 1974

Dear Stephen:

Let me start with my usual apology for having delayed so long in writing.

The news like everything else is a mixture of good and not so good. We are all fortunately in relatively good health.

Mother is somewhat upset over Matthew's progress, or rather the lack of it, in school. We lost our tempers over it.

Riley has emerged from the basement. Mother thinks he has made progress. I must agree. He now wants to go abroad which I don't find amiss, but I don't know what he or I can do about money. (It's too late to bemoan the past; he could have earned money, but of course he was in too unsettled a mental state.) As of yesterday, he'd like to leave in July – I think.

As you may have heard, Melanie, Riley and Mother have been "disfellowshipped" by the Witnesses. Peter is still in good standing. They are still believers in the message they preach.

Our marriage seems to be foundering. I think Mother would like me to leave. Indeed, both she and Riley have suggested it. It's sad that we have come to such a pass, but that's how it is.

I meant to begin this letter with telling you how we are looking forward to your visit. Take care of yourself.

All my love,

Daddy

Well-educated, our father had graduated first in his class and Phi Beta Kappa in German from West Virginia University. He obtained a master's degree at Columbia University in New York City, worked on his doctorate in the German cities of Heidelberg and Marburg in the 1930's, and taught English in Puerto Rico. He was an editorial assistant on the staff of the Middle English Dictionary. During World War II, as a member of the Army's Counter Intelligence Corps, he was part of a top-secret Investigation of Nazi Activities in Heidelberg University. He had been sent by ESSO Oil Co. to Libya to teach English to the heir apparent in preparation for a visit to America. When he met our mother in 1947, he was head of the German department at Stephen's College in Missouri. Our father also spoke or knew six languages: Arabic, English, French, German, Spanish, and Latin. Yet in his sixties he could not find a job.

Some years earlier, in 1961, our family had been living in Charleston, South Carolina, where our father was the Assistant Professor of Modern Language, French and German, at the College of Charleston. He loved it there and would probably have been happy to spend the rest of his life in Charleston. The warmth, for one (he always hated the cold after fighting in the Battle of the Bulge) and the pace of a smaller city, all appealed to him. So why did we leave? Tenure. Or rather the lack of it. Our father had been offered a raise but not tenure for his sixth year at the College—he had not fulfilled the college's PhD requirement. While this was the policy of the school, our father took the decision as a personal insult and decided to leave Charleston because of it. In November the whole family, including we two-month old twins, moved back to D.C., where our parents had lived during the early years of their marriage, in-between their stints overseas. This may have sown the seeds for our mother's ultimate disdain of higher education. She felt that our father was more than qualified to be offered tenure, that he had proved these qualifications every day during his five years of teaching, and the fact that the college would turn him down showed that it had become bogged down in "rules for the sake of rules."

In Washington, they rented a home in Georgetown while our father searched for work. Unable to get a job with the government—they had hoped for an opportunity in the Middle East—he found, through a friend, employment at the University of Tampa in Florida. For the next three years he lived in Tampa during the school year, returning to D.C. and the new home they had bought in Foxhall Village during the summers. Eventually, unable to decide whether to move the family to Florida, our father left the Tampa job and returned to Washington. He never found secure work afterwards.

Taking odd jobs here and there, from selling subscriptions to the Evening Star to working in the menswear department in the bargain basement of Hecht's department store, he continued looking for a teaching position. Finally, an opportunity arose as a substitute teacher in the District of Columbia public-school system. As part of the hiring process the schools required a physical exam. Our father made an appointment at the Veterans Administration, where doctors found a spot on one of his lungs. They determined it was cancer (smaller in size than the head of a pin), and surgery was deemed necessary. When our father came home from that visit to the doctor, we had a family meeting about the operation. Most of us said we did not want him to have the surgery—he appeared so healthy to us, why do it? Also, Annie

Laurie had been greatly affected by having read *Back to Eden*, a book advocating healthy eating as a means of preventing and curing most illnesses, and we are sure this was influential in her antipathy towards the surgery. The rest of us dutifully echoed her. Only Peter had the wisdom to say he did not know enough about the problem to offer an opinion. In any event, after much deliberation, our father went in for the surgery, which he survived. But a year later, in 1974, more cancer was discovered, and he returned to the hospital for a second operation.

At this point, because Farris was not doing well, Annie Laurie called his siblings. Two came to visit him, his younger brother Victor and a younger sister Helen. Throughout the years, our mother seemed to be a little resentful of our father's relationship with his siblings. This sentiment even extended to his deathbed, when his sister leaned over and whispered something to our father that she did not want our mother to hear. For years this bothered Annie Laurie, though as our family went through subsequent adventures she began to understand that perhaps their closeness was due to the shared experience of growing up the children of immigrants.

Although our father's mother had given birth to fourteen children, only eight lived to maturity. On one of the few occasions when our father talked about his childhood, he spoke of his twin siblings Amin and Amina. One had died of the cold at the age of two or three, and the other, he said, of a broken heart not long afterwards. We did not realize at the time—we were probably about ten when he told us this while we were helping him fold socks—how tragic this must have been. God, how we would love to talk to him now, with the perspective of age. But as our mother used to say, "The only way to go backwards is to go forwards."

The surviving siblings of our father rose from poverty and went on to acquire multiple undergraduate and graduate degrees, becoming successful in their respective fields. The one thing their father had insisted upon was getting a good education. Though even when attending university, money was tight; our father often spoke of having to choose between a five-cent subway-ride to Columbia University or a five-cent cup of coffee. He always chose the coffee and walked the several miles to school. And once he was so hungry, he had to overcome the temptation to steal a carrot from a produce stand. This experience of cold, hunger, loss and outsider status as immigrant children was something with which our mother simply could not identify. She came from a vastly different background of wealth and belonging. But it may have created a bond between our father and his siblings that she just could not comprehend.

Our father never came out of the hospital after that second operation. He died on July 24, 1974—Paul's tenth birthday.

Farris was buried in Rock Creek Cemetery in Washington, D.C. As we got out of the limousine at the gravesite, uncomfortably self-conscious of the people watching us, we giggled. Oh, this was horrible; not only were people looking at us but here we were laughing instead of crying, and unable to stop it. Years later when we shamefully brought this up, our mother kindly attributed our giggling to nervousness.

Before the casket was lowered into the ground, our mother, wearing white, asked for it to be re-opened so she could look at our father one more time. The casket was then lowered. We returned to the house and held a party on the patio. Annie Laurie never had a gravestone made; whether that was due to financial reasons, or because "Moses is buried in an unmarked grave" we were never certain. Outwardly she was stoic about our father's death and throughout the burial process.

It took a while, almost three months, for the grief to set in for our mother. We would come home from school to find her sobbing, talking to Riley and Melanie, pouring her heart out. She had one regret after another, from putting our father's office space in our windowless basement when he loved the sunlight, to wishing she'd moved their bedroom to the sunny third floor of our home (an unheard-of concept at the time), to regretting not starting a family business of some sort since he had been unable to find a good job. He had been such a strong support for her during the early years of the marriage, when she had suffered from debilitating depression. Her depression was so severe that at one point while living in Germany she had taken a journey alone, contemplating suicide. She returned, unable to go through with her plan. Her depression, she had always told us, never occurred over anything specific. A great black despair just overtook her. And our father had always been there for her, listening, and essentially, as she said, serving as her therapist. Yet she had not been able to support him in his dark hours.

They had had what seemed to us an almost fairy-tale like existence when first married and living in Europe. We often wondered how our mother managed to see to it that our father obtained an overseas assignment soon after they married; she was not about to stay in Missouri and live a humdrum, mundane life as a newly-wed young lady. She wanted to see the world, and see the world she did. Our father was the perfect companion for her—not only had he lived and studied in Germany before the war, he also knew six languages. And she loved how he never embarrassed her in public the way her father had done when she was a child. When upset over a dinner check which had been incorrectly totaled, her father would summon the waiter to his table and give him a very public dressing-down accompanied by a lesson in arithmetic; mortified, she had wanted to disappear. By contrast, our father's savoir faire was extremely attractive to her.

Travelling via ship from the U.S., they lived in Europe on two separate occasions, one time in Berlin, Germany and another time in Salzburg, Austria. From there they not only saw much of Europe, but also visited Lebanon, the homeland of our father's family. She loved those years—skiing in St. Moritz, Switzerland, and enjoying a brandy on the terrace afterwards; in Venice, posing in a gondola on the Grand Canal with the Rialto bridge behind her, and feeding the pigeons in St. Mark's Square; sipping coffee at a café on the Rue Royal in Paris; costume parties in Austria during Fasching; performing with an English acting troupe; plucking olives from a tree in the Holy Land.

Our father enjoyed window shopping, so was a wonderful companion for our mother as they toured the different cities. And when he did not partake in certain activities (skiing, for example!), he was happy to sit at the lodge enjoying a coffee while awaiting her return from the slopes. From the photos we saw it appeared to be a life to which we could never aspire: The clothes! The glamour! They even had a cook and a maid. This was a far cry from the casual world we lived in, and the mother we knew, the one who cooked, cleaned, and raised eight children with no outside help.

And to top it off, people had constantly told them that even after ten years of marriage, they seemed as in love as newlyweds.

Perhaps this was due to the age difference. Some thirteen years older than our mother, our father indulged her every whim, and much like Rhett Butler to Scarlett O'Hara, he introduced her to the cosmopolitan ways of Europe. With his government job, which even paid for their several journeys via ship to and from the States, and her dividend checks from an inheritance from her father, they never lacked for money. Once, when our father gave our mother a gift, she apparently broke down and cried. Not because she did not like the gift, but because she felt she could not respond in kind. Not only had she learned so much from him, but he was her rock . . . and on top of that he gave beautiful gifts. It was, indeed, an outsize romance to our young eyes.

A transformative experience occurred in her mid-thirties, after she suffered a miscarriage. Convinced she had caused it by her smoking, she told the doctor her fears. When he informed her that that was not the case, she felt the power of God's forgiveness, and in that moment our mother came to know, without a shadow of a doubt, that God existed. Her periods of severe depression lifted, never to return. But she always knew and appreciated how much our father's support had helped her come through. (She also felt blessed by God when her next pregnancy resulted in the birth of twins.)

At the time of his cancer diagnosis they had been in a rut, and he died before they could emerge from it. Looking back, it seems to us that he just gave up. Physically, despite the cancer, he had been in excellent health. Slim, he walked everywhere and ate lots of fruits and vegetables when most of America was eating canned foods and TV dinners. Emotionally, however, his health may have been at risk. The marriage had reached a point of needing care, and instead of focusing on her husband, Annie

Laurie seemed to give priority to Riley and Melanie. It was as if the three of them were the leaders in the family, with our father a mere hanger-on.

Now he was gone, and our mother was left a fifty-two-year-old widow with eight children ages nine through twenty-five.

For us, though, we were so sure that our father would be resurrected, and that we would soon see him again as a perfect, healthy man in a paradise on earth, that perhaps we didn't grieve "normally." Who knows? What we do know is that after his death our mother, in her usual determined way, did everything a widow is not supposed to do. She made major decisions within a year of his dying, though again, she did it with such conviction and discussion that we were all on board. Well, maybe not everyone.

Peter had spent the two months immediately following our father's death visiting Stephen in Hawaii, where the two of them biked, went to the beaches, attended the 50th State Fair, enjoyed ballgames, and just spent time together when Stephen was not working. Finally, though, Stephen thought it about time for Peter to return home (he had only bought a one-way ticket), and gently suggested he buy a return ticket, which he did.

Peter was quiet and introspective, as well as industrious. Since he and Stephen had to share a room while Riley and Melanie each got to have their own, they decided to make their room the "cool" one, buying a fish-tank which Peter meticulously cared for, getting themselves a TV, putting up that poster of Raquel Welch. Peter was also the first to get a "grown-up" bicycle, buying himself a five-speed racing bike. He was not as careful as he should have been when he first took it out, though.

Loving the thrill of its speed as he pedaled down Reservoir Road, but unfamiliar with the hand breaks, he tumbled head-over-heels onto the pavement as he tried to slow down. Thank God, the worst that happened was that he lost the tip of his little finger. When the road was paved shortly afterwards, we morbidly wondered if that fingertip was under the blacktop.

While Peter initially had no interest in what Jehovah's Witnesses were teaching, something must have affected him because before our father died, he began a study of the Bible with them. After several months of study, he cut his long, shaggy hair, bought new dress clothes, got a briefcase, and was baptized at sixteen years old. Annie Laurie always expressed dismay about the day Peter got baptized, and how it unfolded. Her frustration had to do with feeling rushed; they had needed a ride to the ceremony, and the driver had hurried them out the door afterwards, giving them no time to really honor the event, or accord it the respect Annie Laurie felt it deserved. And she worried for Peter, because she knew how important a decision it had been for him.

And then, to make matters worse, several months after Peter's baptism, our mother, Riley, and Melanie were kicked out of the Witnesses. This was not a light matter. A disfellowshipped individual is not to be associated with; if living in the same household average day-to-day communication is allowed, but one should not go out of one's way to interact with that person, and certainly discussions about faith are forbidden. Thus, Peter was effectively without a family. Though he could associate with we four younger ones, since we had neither been baptized nor disfellowshipped, we kind of "didn't count." The oldest four had their own dynamic, and we younger four were pretty much irrelevant to them. This may have been why he enjoyed his long stay in Hawaii with Stephen and had not appeared eager to return home. He could freely associate with his brother who had never accepted the Witness teachings to begin with, whereas he essentially could have no association with his other, older family members, believers who had been disfellowshipped.

We cannot imagine the turmoil Peter must have been under—and at the young age of sixteen. He had committed to a faith which he thought was pleasing to his family, only to have the family kicked out of that faith. And then his father died.

It was March 3rd, 1975, the day before Peter turned eighteen, the spring after our father had died, and the predicted year of Armageddon. Peter had left the house at ten in the morning, dressed in his new jacket and slacks and carrying his briefcase. He appeared to be headed to an appointment, according to Riley. By the time we arrived home from school around three-thirty, our mother was worried. He should have been home for lunch. When he had not returned by dinner time, she realized something was seriously amiss. But she decided to wait the night through, hoping he would return home. By morning, with no sign or word from him, she finally called the police. To no avail, however; they could not help. At eighteen years old, Peter was not considered a runaway. She begged—he was seventeen when he left yesterday. But no, too many young people had left home in the 1970's; this wasn't even a blip on their radar. "He'll show up," they said. "Don't worry."

We thought perhaps Peter had gone to Bethel, the Witness headquarters in New York, but there was no response to the inquiries we made. Had he joined the military? Well, we would never know. A recent law had made us unable to investigate; he could only contact us, not vice-versa.

A year after he left, we sold our house in D.C., and for a long time we wondered if he had ever returned there looking for us. We never saw him again.

CHAPTER 5

RESURRECTION

Our mother mourned. For our father, for Peter, for the life that was lost. But slowly she emerged from her depression, and her zest for life began to return. Her theme song became "Before the Parade Passes By" from the musical *Hello, Dolly!* She would play the piano and sing, the two of us belting out the words along with her. Our mother was coming alive again—watch-out, world!

All the things she had failed to do (whether from fear of the authorities or simply paralysis) when our father was alive, well, she was going to do them now. Losing her husband released a furor that compelled her to action. Come fall, home-schooling would begin. The public schools were a disgrace, she had learned from her study of the Bible that God gave her the authority to teach her children . . . in short, it was the right thing to do. This was a decision she did not come to lightly; a big believer in public education, it was hard for her to admit that the schools had failed. But boy, when she came to that realization, there was no going back. The living and dining rooms were set up as classrooms, complete with easels, blackboards, and armchair desks. We even had a name: The Academy of Semitic Studies—ASS. She loved poking fun at acronym crazy D.C.

We also needed some income. Deciding to refuse both Veterans Benefits and Social Security—she was dependent upon Jehovah, not the U.S. Government—she transformed the garage into a shop of sorts, full of items from our home. Everything was going. The vintage silver and maps of Europe bought after the war. Our father's collection of books, including his Encyclopedia Britannica. The furniture. Even her prized Bechstein grand piano, brought over from Germany. A classified ad placed in the Washington Post brought many interested buyers, including the author Larry McMurtry. We always loved to boast about that.

The financial situation was touch-and-go for a while. At one point, we had no money for groceries. Our mother sat us all down that morning and explained the situation. "We are going to have to have faith that Jehovah will provide," she said. "We'll fast for twenty-four hours and pray that He will help us." Despite the disfellowshipping, her faith in the truth of the Bible was unwavering. And that day, fast we did; from Riley down to eight-year old Matthew, we did not eat for twenty-four hours. Awakening the next morning we gathered in the living room, where Annie Laurie said a prayer. Our day started without breakfast. And then the mail came. In the mail was a check for one-thousand dollars. It was incredible to us, even with our faith, but here it was, tangible proof that Jehovah listened and heard our prayers. And boy, did we rejoice—we broke our fast with fresh fruit, bread, and cheese, bought as soon as we could after cashing the check. And then we composed a celebratory song for the event:

We'll dance in the morning

And we'll dance in the night
Bake our bread, eat our cheese and drink our wine
We'll sing a new song
The good news we'll proclaim
And we'll call God Jehovah by name!

The check had come from Germany. While living in Berlin, our parents had helped a friend by giving her one-thousand German marks. Twenty-five years later, for some reason and completely out-of-the-blue—she had no idea of our current financial straits—that friend had decided to return the funds.

Now while our mother was coming out of her depression and beginning to see a light at the end of the tunnel, others had a different take on things. At the time we had no idea this was going on behind the scenes, but as we later found out, letters, phone calls, and visits were flying back and forth between relatives, neighbors and government officials, all in turmoil about our mother's behavior. It was not long before school officials and social workers were knocking on the door, insisting that our mother register and send us to school. When she declined, one of them suggested she fill out a form requesting permission to teach her children at home. As it dawned on our mother that this had always been a possibility, she almost had a conniption fit, as we used to say. What? It was actually possible to legally teach your children at home? Why hadn't she been aware of this? Well, it was too late now. The schools had failed in their job to educate her children and were in no position to "grant" her the authority to teach them. Her authority came from God.

"Get out of my house!"

CHAPTER 6

WAR

As much fun as we had turning our garage into an antique store, and our first floor into classrooms, that was nothing compared to what we were about to experience. Not long after the visit from the social worker, our mother received a letter. "Well, don't you love this," she said. "It's a summons to appear in court. And in typical government fashion they can't even spell my name right. Well, if they can't bother to get my name right, I'm not going. They can come and get me." And that is exactly what they did.

The day she failed to appear in court two policeman knocked on our door, asked for our mother, and then attempted to hustle her out to the waiting police car. "Can I just get my purse?" she asked. Nope, she had to leave with them immediately. As we tried to follow our mother out the door one of the cops held up his hand to stop us. Escorted down the front steps by the policemen, our mother looked over her shoulder and called to us: "Call a taxi and bring me my purse!" Turning to go back into the house we noticed the neighbors peering out the windows of their homes; no one had come to help us.

With that our battle against "the system" began. It was us against them, and we had the strength of our mother's conviction on our side. And Jehovah. Talk about a dynamic duo—who could withstand that?!

We met our mother's court-appointed lawyer that day, Roger Fore, as well as the Corporation Council—the enemy!— Fred Nussell. Mr. Fore, about twenty-five, was dark-haired, handsome, and earnest. As a recent law school graduate he desperately tried to get our mother to see reason, but his pleas were no match for a woman on a mission. Mr. Nussell, in his mid-thirties, carried himself with an air of worldliness. With a full head of curly hair and a bushy mustache, he could have been an overgrown leprechaun. But not in our eyes. Oh, how we came to loathe this man who was tearing our family apart.

We four minor children were also assigned our own lawyer, Nadine Farring.

Each one of us responded to the judge by stating our name and/or occupation, and then the case started. Forthwith, some of the testimony:

> THE COURT: All right. This matter had been called this morning. A summons had been issued for Mrs. Mansour to appear and she did not appear. Why was that, Mrs. Mansour?
>
> ANNIE LAURIE: Well, for one thing the summons-- my name was incorrect on the summons. And I'm not quite sure what the paper was that was delivered to me.

THE COURT: Didn't the officer tell you that you were to appear here when he handed you this paper? Didn't he tell you that?

ANNIE LAURIE: I believe he did; yes.

THE COURT: And you just ignored it and chose not to come?

ANNIE LAURIE: Yes; I did.

THE COURT: Why is that?

RILEY: The reason Mrs. Mansour did not appear in Court is for this reason, and this explains fully why we do not recognize the jurisdiction of this court: "Jehovah is our Judge; Jehovah is our statute giver; Jehovah is our King. He himself will save us." So we do not recognize this Court— Jehovah is our Judge, and he is the Judge that we recognize.

THE COURT: All right. Do you understand the consequences of ignoring the Court order?

RILEY: We do.

THE COURT: Do you (addressed to Annie Laurie) understand the consequences of ignoring the Court order?

ANNIE LAURIE: I suppose I do.

THE COURT: What is your position about abiding by any future Court orders; do you take the same view that your son takes that you are going to ignore them as you apparently ignored this one?

ANNIE LAURIE: If any order orders me to go against my religious belief, I would do that.

THE COURT: My specific question is if an order is issued to you to appear here in Court, are you going to abide by that order?

ANNIE LAURIE: That depends.

THE COURT: Mr. Foore, I suggest that you had better consult with your client.

MR. FOORE: I have attempted Your Honor; I'll try again.

THE COURT: Because I want to make it clear that she is narrowing my options considerably.

MR. FOORE: I understand that, Your Honor; I'm getting a nervous stomach.

THE COURT: There have been neglect petitions filed here; the allegations are that these children are not going to school. It's a violation of the District of Columbia law for them to be staying out of school, all these children who are under sixteen years of age.

The neglect petition is based upon the fact that you are not sending them to school. A summons was issued for you, Mrs. Mansour, to appear here this morning, and you did not appear. Now, if it's necessary for me to incarcerate you and place these children into the custody of the District officials so that they go to school, I'm going to do it. I'm hoping I don't have to take that extreme step; but, believe me, if I have to take it, I will take it. The reason I don't want to take that extreme step is not out of any compassion for you but out of compassion for these children.

I'll take a recess; you talk to her.

MR. FOORE: Thank you, Your Honor.

We took a break, and after Mr. Foore, our mother's court appointed lawyer, pretty much begged her to at least *say* she would obey a court order, we returned to the courtroom.

THE COURT: All right, Mr. Foore

MR. FOORE: All right, Your Honor. I think my client is ready to answer your question.

THE COURT: All right, Mrs. Mansour

ANNIE LAURIE MANSOUR: Yes, sir.

THE COURT: "Yes sir", what?

ANNIE LAURIE MANSOUR: I will appear in the Court when I am summoned.

THE COURT: All right. Now Mr. Nussell, what is the position of the Government at this point?

MR. NUSSELL: Your Honor, the Government would request the Court set a trial date in this matter in the first week of January; that the Court allow the children to remain with their mother pending the trial date; and that the mother be ordered to enroll the children in school between now and then.

THE COURT: Mr. Foore?

MR. FOORE: Thank you, Judge. I would agree with Mr. Nussell's recommendation with the exception of the requirement of the compulsory school attendance. It's already late November; if we have a trial date in January then we will at that point be able to determine whether this woman is qualified to teach her own children.

THE COURT: She might very well be able to demonstrate that she is qualified, but our concern at this point is that the children get some type of education. For her to say that she is qualified is rather self-serving. We don't accept that from anyone else; we can't accept it from her. So I'm willing to go along with the recommendation providing that the D.C. compulsory school attendance law is complied with, and that can be complied with by them going to a public school, private school or Mrs. Mansour completing the application and getting it approved for her to be a private tutor pending trial.

Is she willing to do that?

Mr. Foore consults with our mother, to no avail.

MR. FOORE: Your Honor, I have talked with the mother, and she is not agreeable to sending them to school or filling out the form.

THE COURT: All right.

Do you have somebody in this area who is head of the church, or somebody you look to for advice as far as your religion is concerned?

MRS. MANSOUR: The Bible.

THE COURT: You have nobody who heads up any formal church organization?

MRS. MANSOUR: I would have to say no.

THE COURT: I am willing to grant a short continuance in this case to give Mrs. Mansour an opportunity to discuss this matter with church officials, even though she says they don't exist. But if she wants to discuss this and come back the first of the week and give us her decision, I'm willing to do that.

MR. FOORE: Your Honor, I would like to have the week-end to discuss in much greater details the ramifications with Mrs. Mansour and her family. I would like to have a further chance to sit down and talk with her at greater length.

THE COURT: Any objections to that?

MR. NUSSELL: No, Your Honor.

MISS FARRING [Children's attorney]: My only comment is that I have had the distinct feeling from talking with the children, as little as I have talked to them, which is not very much, that they rather look upon this hearing as something of a joke, and I should certainly appreciate the Court's explaining to them that the laws of the District of Columbia are not jokes.

THE COURT: Well, I have seen a lot of smiles here this afternoon on their faces, but I can assure them that if I have to take the step which is indicated, that they won't be laughing, because it means they will be separated from their parents; they will be taken out of their home; they will be living in somebody else's home or else some institution; and they will be going to school, probably not a school they would choose if they had some say in the matter. So they would be separated from their mother, brother and sister, and I'm positive that after they are in that setting for a very short time that they would not have any smiles on their faces. I would hope between now and next Tuesday that Mrs. Mansour will talk with her lawyer; that she will talk with individuals in the church because I am satisfied that she has no First Amendment right, no religious right or right of any type to keep these children out of school.

MR. NUSSELL: Can we set a trial date, Your Honor?

THE COURT: What date do you suggest?

MR. NUSSELL: January 5th, Your Honor?

THE COURT: Is that agreeable Mr. Foore?

MR. FOORE: Yes, it is. Your Honor, may my client make a statement to the Court?

THE COURT: Well, it's up to her, as long as she understands that anything she says could very well be used against her.

MRS. MANSOUR: Yes, I understand. Miss Farring, I deeply regret your comments about the children and the smiles on their faces. Of all the things that have occurred to me in twenty years, I don't know of a remark that has more deeply hurt me, and I apologize for any smile on any of my chidren's faces that seemed as if they were not respectful of the Court.

THE COURT: She has only stated what is obvious to everyone here, Mrs. Mansour. You saw the smiles on their faces.

MRS. MANSOUR: People can smile when they are nervous.

THE COURT: But the smiles were there, weren't they?

MRS. MANSOUR: Perhaps they were nervous.

THE COURT: Perhaps they were.

MRS. MANSOUR: I'm very sorry.

Thereupon, at approximately 3:25 p.m., the proceedings in the above-mentioned action were concluded.

We are all re-assembled in the courtroom the next week; our court-appointed lawyer had tried to get our mother to see reason, but she stood firm in her convictions. This hearing took place in front of a new judge, so the Corporation Council had to re-explain the case.

THE COURT: Why is it alleged that the children have not attended school?

MR. NUSSELL: Your Honor, may I make some representations?

THE COURT: Yes

MR. NUSSELL: Your Honor, there is a lengthy background on this case. They have not gone to school because the mother will not send them to school. She will not send them to public school, private school—

THE COURT: Why?

MR. NUSSELL: Your Honor, she is a Jehovah's Witness. The family are Jehovah's Witnesses. They are, apparently, a peculiar kind of Jehovah's Witnesses, if you will. In fact, I believe they are actually ex-communicated Jehovah's Witnesses. That is, they maintain—I'm not sure I'm competent to really represent their views, but the best I can determine is that they are cutting all ties with the temporal world. I think that's a fair statement.

THE COURT: I know we've had this with the Amish, but this isn't—

MR. NUSSELL: This is clearly distinguishable from that, your Honor. If I may just one further thing, Your Honor.

THE COURT: Yes.

MR. NUSSELL: The other complication to this is that the mother, along with the twenty-five year old son who lives in the home and the twenty-one year old daughter who lives in the home, have decided, one, that they will accept no Social Security or Veterans Benefits due to the family; and, number two, that in order to make do on a day to day basis, they have sold out most of the things from the first floor of their house as well as china, silverware and all the rest of it, and they apparently are behind on their mortgage payments, their water bill and their electric bill and their gas bill. And --

THE COURT: This is a sudden change.

MR. NUSSELL: This is the same family. Your Honor, it's a change that's occurred, apparently, over the summer. The husband died in July of '74 and apparently this has sort of been building. I think the seeds of this problem have been there for a long time, but with the absence of the husband . . . he provided a rudder for the family.

In my judgment, the lady is simply unbalanced and incapable of discharging her affairs and handling the family finances or doing anything in a responsible way towards the children.

THE COURT: Mr. Foore?

MR. FOORE: Well, of course, she would take a great deal of issue in that. She's a very articulate and well-spoken lady, who at one time was a college professor in Speech and English at Stephen's College, in Columbia, Missouri. That's where she met her husband, who also was a college professor there. He specialized in German and French languages.

THE COURT: Well, Mr. Nussell, have you seen the house?

MR. NUSSELL: Yes, Your Honor, I have been in the house.

THE COURT: Clean and so forth, just bare?

MR. NUSSELL: The house is clean. The problem is that the only furniture that is in the house at this time, if my recollection serves me, is a piano on the left. To the right there was a table with some wooden chairs, and in the dining room there was a blackboard on the wall and an easel with some maps and five or six of the wooden school-type chairs with the wooden handles that come around on them. She's instructing in the home.

THE COURT: She's instructing the children?

MR. NUSSELL: Yes, but she simply refuses to fill out the application for tutoring at home, which apparently the school system will accept in an emergency basis, even to be in compliance between now and the trial date. I would suggest, your Honor, that at the trial, this matter will show that this lady is mentally unbalanced.

THE COURT:Mr. Foore, where do we stand on these cases?

MR. FOORE: Well, Your Honor, according to Annie Laurie Mansour, the mother, she does not desire to send her children to school because of a certain belief which she holds and, secondly, she disagrees with the requirement of the Government for her to fill out an application showing herself capable to teach her children. She feels that she is, in fact, capable and she's done a very good job of it.

And she opposes, basically, the compulsory school law because of the condition of the District of Columbia schools.

She believes, in short, that she can provide a much better education for her children than the authorities can, and that the Bible provides her a basic authority for her position. I believe that this is also the position of her son, who has sort of stepped in to be the spokesperson for the family, since his father is dead. I think that later on he would perhaps like to tell Your Honor what it is that their philosophy is.

THE COURT: I'm willing to hear it now. Would you identify yourself for the record.

(Now as we four were sitting listening to this, we couldn't wait for Riley to testify. He had come up with the perfect defense—extraterritoriality. A week before we had never even heard the word, but now life as we knew it was dependent upon it. You tell 'em, Riley!)

RILEY: I'm Riley Mansour, the oldest brother of my siblings.

It is claimed by the defense that the Superior Court of the District of Columbia Intra-Family and Neglect Branch does not have jurisdiction in this case. It is further claimed that the judicial body which does have jurisdiction is the body of Elders of Lake Valley congregation of Jehovah's Witnesses in Washington, D.C.

In proof we cite the law stated in Isaiah 33:22, "Jehovah is our judge. Jehovah is our statute giver. Jehovah is our King. He himself will save us."

The defense brings to the Court's attention the fact that Mrs. Mansour is not a citizen of the United States of America according to the Immigration and Nationality Act of 1952. In view of the foregoing statement,—

THE COURT: Where is she a citizen?

RILEY: Jehovah's Kingdom

THE COURT: Oh.

RILEY: In view of the foregoing statements, the defendant claims the privilege of extraterritoriality according to the rules of international law, to wit, "A diplomat cannot be arrested for any reason. His residence, papers, and effects cannot be searched or seized. His personal belongings cannot be taxed by the country in which he serves. He, his family and his staff enjoy complete freedom of worship."

That is our statement to the Court.

THE COURT: Do you wish to elaborate any further, Mr. Mansour?

RILEY: Yes, just this—it is claimed by the defense that the free exercise of religion as enumerated in the First Amendment to the United States Constitution is by definition absolute and not relative. Relative free exercise of religion is an abridgment thereof.

That is the only added thing we have to say to the Court.

THE COURT: Just a few questions for you. I am told you are all members of Jehovah's Witnesses; is that right?

(Family nods, affirmatively)

Is that the Witnesses' general tenet and belief, that children do not attend public school?

RILEY: No.

THE COURT: May I ask you, then, what request you are making of the court? I know of cases involving the Amish, but I know in that situation, that was a very strong and well-known part or tenet of their belief. I do not know of any such tenet with respect to Jehovah's Witnesses.

I also must keep in mind the best welfare of these children, for them, though I must say, as an aside, they certainly are a fine-looking family. I certainly commend you on this family.

RILEY: I would like to bring to the Court's attention that Jehovah's Witnesses preach that Jehovah's Kingdom was established in 1914 and that since that date the Kingdom of God is ruling. We do then owe allegiance to this Kingdom of God, and thus, according to the act of 1952 have been stripped of our United States citizenship. So that, according to the principle of extraterritoriality, we request that the Court dismiss the action since we are not under the laws of the United States.

THE COURT: Sir, please forgive my ignorance, because I must confess that I do not know an awful lot about your religion. I am acquainted with people who are, and I have friends who are Jehovah's Witnesses, but I do not wish that to sound like I'm saying "Some of my friends are Jehovah's Witnesses", but where in your faith do you place the Trinity or Christ?

RILEY: We do not believe in the Trinity. We believe in Jesus as the Son of God.

THE COURT: And do you believe in the Gospels that are set forth in the Bible?

RILEY: Yes.

THE COURT: Now, Mr. Nussell stated earlier that you are excommunicated from the Jehovah's Witnesses. Is that correct?

RILEY: It is. However, we still hold their interpretation of Scripture to be accurate.

THE COURT: So, even though you were kicked out, as it were, you still adhere to their beliefs?

RILEY: Yes.

THE COURT: Well, let me ask you this. My immediate problem is what happens between now and when this decision can be decided in court. Do you have any suggestions for the Court?

RILEY: We request that until the trial we be allowed to obtain jurisdiction over the children and that my mother be allowed to keep her freedom. We request that we be allowed to remain together as a family.

MR. NUSSELL: Your Honor, if I may be heard. As I said before, I think that the problem the Court is confronted with is substantially more far-reaching than simply not placing the minors in school. And the response of the Mansours, as I understand it, is simply that "Jehovah will provide". I suggest that the Court may at some point have to step in as an instrument of Jehovah, if you will, and take some action because I think they are in imminent danger of losing their home and living in a condition that's quite honestly intolerable, to be put into the street.

I would suggest, Your Honor, having heard the testimony of Mr. Mansour, that the Court place the four children in the custody of the Department of Human Resources at this time, and that the Court enter an order that the four children be evaluated psychiatrically at Children's Hospital pending the trial date.

MR. FOORE: Your Honor, I would oppose the breakup of this family. This is a very close-knit family.

THE COURT: Well, what concerns me, though, is that it's not just a problem of school. Now, what's going to happen to these children if the family is not accepting funds to support themselves—

How are you supporting yourselves, if I may ask?

RILEY: Well, we've been following Jesus' instruction to sell our possessions and we've been proceeding to do this.

THE COURT: What happens when you have sold everything and lost your home?

RILEY: Our position with the Court is that the children are being fed at the moment. Mr. Nussell is speaking of an action that might happen in the future. But the real question before the Court is whether the children are in immediate danger, and until there is actual evidence that the children have been mistreated, we ask that the Court refrain from taking custody of the children.

THE COURT: Is it not a possible danger that you will lose your home?

You see, we reach a point, I'm afraid, where the State has to intervene because these four children are not of age.

RILEY: Due to the nature of the case, we argue that we owe allegiance to another sovereign and that while under law, it is not the law of the United States. That is why we ask that you turn us over to Jehovah's Witnesses, whom we do recognize as having authority over us.

We do not claim to be above the law. In this case it is a matter of whose law.

THE COURT: Sir, to your knowledge, and I have to rely upon your answer, do you know of anyone who is a part of the Jehovah's Witnesses faith which support your viewpoints? You know, it's easy for someone to just walk out of the door and proclaim his own religion. Is this really a tenet of your religion? I take it it is not.

RILEY: I would argue that we believe the teachings of the Witnesses and are following what they have said to its logical conclusion.

Our point is that the United States, if it wishes, may either drop the charges on the issue of extraterritoriality, or may deport us. But that we are acting as ambassadors from another country and are therefore not subject to all of the laws of the United States.

THE COURT: You're taking it beyond what the Jehovah's Witnesses suggested, though; is that it?

RILEY: Well, they suggest that the "Gentile" times ended in 1914-

THE COURT: Excuse me—what does "Gentile" times mean?

RILEY: It's a lease of power granted by God to Gentile rulers on earth, and that lease ended in 1914.

THE COURT: Oh. Well, first, let me make this statement. You have given the Court two choices. One is either to exile you, I suppose, or, the other is to dismiss the case. Of course, I am sure you realize those are two choices that the Court cannot really exercise.

RILEY: There are questions of international law in view of the nature of the case itself; we owe allegiance to another sovereign. We are under law, but not the law of the United States.

THE COURT: You do not believe in the statement that you render unto Caesar that which is Caesar's?

RILEY: That was until the Gentile times ended, in 1914. This is the belief of the Witnesses.

THE COURT: What is the option I have?

RILEY: Well, we can make a case to the Court that the children are not neglected because that question of whether the children are neglected involves the question of whether Jehovah is in neglect of the children. Any questions or complaints raised about the way Jehovah runs the universe, which is the fundamental issue which is involved here, is a very serious charge, and this is a very live issue that has been going on throughout human history. Jehovah would like to answer the charges.

The issue isn't so much whether my mother is neglectful; she is merely a representative of Jehovah and doing what she thinks Jehovah wants.

THE COURT: Anything else, Mr. Nussell?

MR. NUSSELL: Your Honor, first, it seems important—whether Mrs. Mansour adopts everything that has been said in regard to these matters.

I think that is important for the record.

THE COURT: Do you, Mrs. Mansour?

MRS. MANSOUR: Yes, I do, Judge

MR. NUSSELL: Your Honor, I think that Mrs. Mansour, through Riley Mansour, has made herself and himself abundantly clear that they have no intention, whatsoever, of complying with the compulsory education

law. I think that, on its face, is contemptuous conduct. I
think additionally important, and perhaps more importantly
in terms of talking about the children and their welfare, is
the other problem that I mentioned that I intend to
incorporate into a petition. I simply cannot, in good
conscience, stand by while this family loses a house which I
would suggest to the Court is valued somewhere in the
neighborhood of in excess of $75,000, when they could be
accepting Social Security benefits and Veterans Benefits.

I've thought about this a great deal in terms of the
course of action that I would take, and I simply decided that
I could not stand by and wait until the family found itself in
the street, and then come in when there was some
opportunity to be involved with the family.

I might add that the problem is not subject to an
easy resolution.

I know that the Family and Child Services social
worker has had three or four visits with the family to discuss
the various problems. I know that Twenty-Four Hour
Protective Services made one visit to the home, I know that
the Social Services Branch of the Department of Human
Resources made four or five home visits, the schools'
attendance officers and social workers have made three or
four visits to the house in trying to deal with this particular
problem.

Her response, basically, is that Jehovah will provide.
I simply pose to the Court that the Court cannot adopt or
endorse that kind of view at this particular time.

I would urge the Court, again, to place these
children in foster homes.

THE COURT: Mr. Foore?

MR. FOORE: All right, Your Honor. I will not, at the outset, address myself to the allegations that Mr. Nussell has made with regard to financial problems the family may have.

I would like to say that I think to remove these children from the household of this close-knit family would be a grave mistake.

THE COURT: Where would the children be placed if I were to place them in shelter care? Do we have a facility for them right now, and can we keep them together; is that possible?

MRS. FERGMAN [social worker]: We would not be able to keep all four together. We would be able to keep the two boys together, and the two girls together in another home.

THE COURT: Can I have the assurance that no one in the shelter care setting will in any way attempt to disturb their beliefs up to this point?

MRS. FERGMAN: Certainly.

THE COURT: Because if I should remove them from the home, I do not want to disturb what their beliefs might be, except, of course, they may have to go to school. Are there any other alternatives that we have that either the Government or the social worker can present to the Court?

MR. NUSSELL: No, Your Honor.

THE COURT: I think there has been a request by Mr. Nussell for an examination. Is that right?

MR. NUSSELL: Yes.

THE COURT: Well, if that is being requested by the District Attorney, I would order that the children be examined.

May I have counsel at the bench for a moment, and the social worker?

Thereupon, counsel for both sides, and the social worker approach the bench and confer with the Court in low tones of voice, as follows:

THE COURT: Do we have any other alternatives that you can suggest? Mr. Nussell, suppose the children were to return home. Do you feel there is a possibility they may flee?

MR. NUSSELL: I hadn't worried about that terribly much before I heard Riley Mansour's presentation about his position vis-a-vis the court, and that leads me to believe they would leave.

THE COURT: They would?

MR. NUSSELL: They would leave. He views himself as an emissary of some sovereign nation coming down here and appearing before the Court out of some sense of grace, rather than being commanded to be here. I'm not sure the ride in the police car made any difference at all. I think that was just transportation for Mrs. Mansour.

THE COURT: Mr. Foore—

MR. FOORE: I'm almost in an untenable position in this case. I mean, you don't know how many hours I've put in in counseling the family as to why it is the Government is bringing these charges and what it is they can do to shut the Government off. All they have to do is comply, but they absolutely refuse to do anything.

And that's hard for me. I have no legal basis. I've looked up all the legal precedents concerning this and there just seemed no legal foundation for their stand.

I just think it would be terrible for the family if they broke up because they are so very close.

MR. NUSSELL: Your Honor, I've sweat blood over this case trying to figure out what is the right thing to do, and the deeper I get into the case the more I'm convinced we are dealing with people who are extraordinarily mentally troubled people. I just find appalling what is happening. If it were just a school type problem that would be different, but I see, it seems to me, a pathology. If you observe the behavior of this family, you see the two youngest kids, the boys, who are the least involved, you see the twins who are slightly more involved in terms of family conferences, and you see, I think, a very pathological relationship between Riley, Melanie, and the mother.

And I see the four kids, the twins more than the two younger kids, on the borderline of going into this kind of thing where they're going to turn out to be—well, I mean, really bad off people. This is supported by relatives and neighbors. We have provided the Court with letters from concerned relatives, including some from Mrs. Mansour's sisters and brother-in-law.

THE COURT: If they're placed in shelter care, will the mother be able to see them?

MRS. FERGMAN: That's never been a problem.

MR. NUSSELL: I had hoped, when I entered this case, to begin just incrementally, to make some difference, and the more I dug into it the more bizarre things that I found, and I just found it finally intolerable not to take some action. I cannot help but think that these people are acting so irrationally, so bizarre, and so against the interest of the younger children.

THE COURT: I have to step back sometimes, or say, sometimes "I wonder what is bizarre".

When I go up to Lancaster, Pennsylvania, those people certainly act very bizarre under certain circumstances when they would walk around with their long, black outfits on.

MR. NUSSELL: I agree.

THE COURT: But they were expelled from Jehovah's Witnesses, is this a fact?

MR. NUSSELL: They were expelled. I've heard it from other sources and hearing it from Riley it certainly confirms what we've heard before.

THE COURT: Can they be placed today? I would certainly prefer to see them placed right in rather than spend any time—

MRS. FERGMAN: There's a nice home in Maryland for the two little boys, and one in Virginia for the girls.

MR. FOORE: I would just hate to see the children separated, and I'm not altogether sure, when we talk about pathology here, that we're not just talking based upon our own prejudices.

MR. NUSSELL: I would simply suggest it is pathological not to pay your water bills and not to pay your mortgage for the kinds of reasons they're coming up with. (Now, we have to interject here. For what it is worth, our mother told us in later years that the bills were, in fact, paid, and always up to date. The house was never under foreclosure. And years after she died, we found a letter from the water company, which she must have requested, indicating that at no time was the water ever scheduled to be turned off for late or non-payment. So, some of what the prosecutor was hearing from neighbors must have been pure conjecture.)

MR. NUSSELL: I would like to have the mother evaluated, but I think at this stage of the proceedings it's pushing it a little far.

THE COURT: I'm afraid so.

MR. NUSSELL: But I just think, in the conversations I've had with people—her sister on Long Island, several neighbors that have contacted me—that have had contact with the family, and just my impressions from seeing the family in operation, it's kind of a frightening prospect to see these kids who are all bright-eyed and bushy-tailed slowly going downhill.

THE COURT: Okay. Let's get to it. God—or should I say Jehovah—help us if Riley is right and we are wrong. I'm in big trouble.

Thereupon, the proceedings at the bench are concluded; all persons in attendance return to their respective positions in the well of the courtroom and the proceedings continue-

CLERK: All parties, please, in the Mansour case, would you come back before the Court?

THE COURT: Mr. Mansour, just to confirm—you are not willing, as I understand it, between now and the time of any hearing, to see to it that the children are presented for examination by psychologists and psychiatrists according to my order; is that right?

RILEY: Yes, it is.

THE COURT: All right. Well, this, of course, is a very difficult situation for the Court to be placed in. It is easier not to be here, of course, than to be here but the Court, nevertheless, has to make decisions.

I believe, as Mr. Mansour said in his explanation to the Court, they have their duty and, indeed, the Court has its duty. The Court must act in a way in which it will protect what it feels is the best interests of these children.

Taking everything into consideration, based upon the statements of the family here, I am just afraid that this Court has no choice but to have the children placed in temporary shelter care.

I will order a psychological and psychiatric examination for each of the children.

The Court is not trying in any way to disrupt this family. It's the last thing I have in my mind. But, the Court feels that it must act at this time in the best interests of these children as it sees it, and I am not going to sit here and claim that I am in any way infallible—but I must act as I see what their best interests might be. I will order that they be placed in temporary shelter care, but, in addition to that, I want them placed as soon as possible in a group home, group setting, or foster home. Are there any questions about the order of the Court from anyone?

I take it there are no questions. I know it's difficult for the children, I know it's difficult for you, but I will do everything in my power to see that they are as comfortable as possible.

Thereupon, at 4:45 pm, the proceedings conclude.

Wait . . . what?! We could not believe we were being taken away. What was happening? But our mother assured us that this was a battle for Jehovah, and we were on the front lines. She would work on getting all the backing necessary to fight a successful battle. Her strength and conviction were powerful—despite being taken away we never doubted her concern for us.

CHAPTER 7

FRONT LINES

After the hearing, with nothing but the clothes on our backs, and despite the assurance that foster homes were available, we twins were taken to the Girard Street shelter for girls in downtown Washington, D.C. Arriving after dark, we were led upstairs to a room with bunkbeds, and given nightgowns. The steam-pipe sizzling next to our bed kept us awake half the night; though cold outside, the window was wide open to alleviate the heat.

While getting dressed the following morning we chatted with our six black roommates. They were getting ready for school and were ironing their clothes on the bed, rather than using an ironing board. (We had never seen that done before and thought it ingenious.) "Are you coming to school with us? Why are you here?" they asked. "Well, of course we're not going to school," we replied, "that's why we're here." Following a breakfast of a banana and milk—we turned up our noses at the gross looking eggs and sausages—we made a phone call to our mother. And boy, we could not believe the news—Paul and Matthew were home! What had happened? We heard quite a tale.

The boys, nine and eleven-years-old, had been placed in a hospital overnight. Stripped of their clothes, dressed in hospital gowns, and given medicine (what it was and for what reason, we were never able to find out),they were put to bed in a patient room. The next morning, none of the staff knew what to do with them. As they wandered the hallways in hospital gowns, Paul insisted to a nurse that their clothes be returned. They were finally found in a closet. The boys dressed, and, with no-one paying any attention, left the hospital. Walking from South-East to North-West Washington, D.C., they found their way home in time for breakfast.

Here is our mother's take on the episode. "Well, that hospital staff must have been petrified when the social worker called to ask about the boys, and they were nowhere to be found. The police had to be called and two very nice officers showed up at our house this morning. I began telling them all about the case and I do think they found it fascinating. You know, girls, the one officer asked me to play 'What a friend we have in Jesus' on the piano before they had to leave with the boys. I'm telling you, this case is much bigger than anyone realizes."

As soon as we heard the news of the boys, we looked at each other and wondered "why didn't we think of that?" We immediately decided to copy them. Peeking around the corner of the telephone room we saw the caretaker busy in her office. We snuck past, ran upstairs to get our coats, and just as rapidly tiptoed back down. If the caretaker saw us leave, we would tell her we were taking a walk; thankfully, she did not notice us. We ran to the corner to get out of sight, then paused to consider which way to go. While we were not in a familiar neighborhood, we had walked so much in the downtown area when with our family that we knew that if we found a recognized landmark, we would know which path to follow. After a few false starts, we committed to one direction. When we passed Francis Pool, the public swimming pool to which our family walked weekly, if not more often, during the summers, our hearts lifted. *Now* we were in familiar territory. The last two miles of our four-mile walk home lay ahead, but we did not mind in the least, having confirmation that we were headed in the right direction.

Our mother and Melanie could not believe it when they saw us, and they eagerly listened as we proudly told our tale. Annie Laurie made us a delicious dinner before we climbed, exhausted, into bed. Oh, how comforting it felt to be home.

Soon we heard the wail of a police siren. Oh, no, had they found us already? We stayed in bed until our mother came up, informing us we had to go back. Getting dressed, we dutifully followed the policemen in the dark to the waiting police-car and were taken back to the Girard Street shelter. It would be years before we could hear a siren without flinching. The next day we were driven from the shelter to our new "home," a foster house in suburban Manassas, Virginia.

We hated everything about it. On a country road with no sidewalks (a serious affront to us who walked everywhere), it was a modest ranch house with doors that couldn't even be slammed shut in anger (and boy, were we angry) they were so flimsy. We were placed in a room with one bed—really? We have to share a bed? How is that better than home, where we each have our *own* bed?

Our foster mother, Mrs. Freedon, was mousy, serious, timid, and cheap; we never much cared for her. Mr. Freedon, on the other hand, was gregarious and full of life. He tried hard to please us, bringing us milkshakes and burgers from Hardees, or driving us down the road to see his cattle, or teasing us by asking to shake hands when he came home from work covered in mechanics' grease. But we refused to warm up. This was not home and never would be.

It was not until a week after we were removed from her custody that our mother finally found out where everyone was. Paul and Matthew had been taken to a foster home in Huntingtown, Maryland.

Dec. 10, 1975

Dear Paul and Matthew,

Only yesterday evening did the social worker tell us where you and Matthew were—and she wasn't exactly sure this is the correct address!

We received a letter from Maryam!! We had no idea where they were. We wrote them two long letters—they asked for your address—I must write them NOW your address—but how I wish it were complete. They are with a couple named Mr. & Mrs. Freedon.

There are many things we want to write you but this first letter is to let you know we are thinking of you and missing you and Matthew very much. It's too quiet around here!

We want you to be good witnesses wherever you are and whatever you may be doing.

Paul—Riley, Melanie and I have been talking for days about how proud we are of your behavior. You have shown great courage and intelligence as the older brother. Be sure you keep an eye on that Matthew!—make sure that his bed does not look as if a hurricane hit it.

Now, Matthew, remember Paul is your older brother and will give you "wise counsel" when necessary. Also—stay away from those fast cars. WALK! wherever you go.

We were told you are in school. That is against our wishes, but if you are forced to go—use your head and be a good witness.

Remember, Jehovah is watching very closely over you and will protect you. Be sure you talk to Him and tell Him everything and He will guide you. He is your Father. Be sure to read all about Paul and Silas in the Bible (Acts 16:25-40) as the Baptist policeman told you. And sing "and we'll call God Jehovah by name!"

Love,

MOTHER,

Melanie!

Riley!

With our hopes glued to the upcoming trial on January 5th, we were able to endure the winter weeks of December with some equanimity. We refused to go to school—wasn't that the whole point of the trial?! (And we thought our speeches to Mrs. Freedon giving our rationale for that decision quite eloquent.) But we tried to keep ourselves busy writing letters both home and to Paul and Matthew in their foster home. We also loved to bake, and that too kept us occupied: bread, oatmeal cookies, cinnamon bread, breadsticks. Being outside was almost a necessity—how we craved fresh air and sunshine, as well as escape from our claustrophobic foster home. And so we walked up and down the lonely, sidewalk-less road, only to be mortified on occasion by the jeering taunts of school-bus riders accusing us of being "street-walkers."

Finally, the trial date arrived. Oh, we were so excited: to be going home! We would never complain about the endless Biblical conversations between Riley, Melanie and our mother again!

CHAPTER 8

TRIAL

January 5th, 1976. The first Monday of the new year. The trial did not begin until almost three o'clock, and the waiting was enough to send our mother on a tirade about the inefficiencies of the "system." Finally, the wait was over. We had yet another judge, though most of the other players remained the same: our mother's lawyer Roger Foore, the Assistant Corporation Council Frank Nussell, we four children's attorney Jeanne Bowers. (Truthfully, she never made much of an impact on us and we never realized we had anyone on "our" side. "On behalf of the Children" must have meant something entirely different to the court system than it did to us children.) The testimony follows:

OPENING STATEMENT ON BEHALF OF THE
GOVERNMENT

MR. NUSSELL: Your Honor, in this case the
Government has petitioned as neglected children the four
youngest Mansour children; the two girls are fourteen years
of age and the two boys are eleven and nine respectively.
The basis of the Government's petition in this case is that
the children, all four of these children are subject to the

compulsory school laws of the District of Columbia and they have not been sent to school this school year by their mother. She is not in compliance with the compulsory school attendance laws which are title 31 Section 201 following of the District of Columbia Code. The children come within the jurisdiction of the Court pursuant to 16 D.C. Code 23019B, that is when children are without proper parental care, control and education as required by law.

That is the basis of the Government's case, and the Government will show by a preponderance that the children are in fact neglected children.

At this point Mr. Nussell called Riley to testify, and he basically reiterated much of what he had spoken about in the hearing. Now it was time for our mother's attorney to make his statement.

THE COURT: Mr. Foore, do you wish to make an opening statement?

MR. FOORE: Yes, Your Honor.

OPENING STATEMENT ON BEHALF OF THE DEFENDANT

MR. FOORE: I would like to start by saying that Mrs. Annie Laurie Mansour, the mother of the four children in question, is not a neglectful mother. She wants to do the best possible thing for her children commensurate with her religious beliefs.

At this point in time her beliefs conflict with the state's regulations with respect to school attendance. Mrs. Mansour believes, and we intend to prove to the Court, that she is a fit and proper custodian of her children and she has the ability and professional background which would enable her to teach her children in her own home.

I hope to show to the Court that there were reasons, which Mrs. Mansour will probably be able to discuss with the Court much better than I can, as to why her children were removed from the public schools and that she does not take lightly her responsibilities in this entire matter, and that she wants and intends to be a good mother for these children. At this point, I call Mrs. Annie Laurie Mansour to the stand.

After answering a long series of questions about her background, the testimony finally came to the part where our mother attempts to explain the reasons behind her decision to home-school.

MR. FOORE: Now, before May of 1975, the last year the children attended public school, had your family had occasion to have discussions about whether it was the proper thing to send the children back to school the following school year?

MRS. MANSOUR: Yes. We had had discussions over a long period of time about the school situation but probably not until the last six months before June did we really begin to think we would take that step.

MR. FOORE: What led to this? Tell the Court what it was that led your family to take this precipitous step that has now caused this whole matter to come to Court. Take your time, please. I know that this is rather overwhelming for you.

MRS. MANSOUR: It is. I have often tried to find a sentence that would describe such a situation in one

sentence. But it's not that simple. You know, I put eight
children through public schools - -

MR. FOORE: Does that include the younger four?

MRS. MANSOUR: Yes, eight children have gone
through the public schools, and in the last fourteen years,
increasingly year by year, the school situation became a little
worse each year.

MR. FOORE: Go ahead, Mrs. Mansour, continue.

MRS. MANSOUR: I have gotten to the point where,
when I am asked this question, I really don't like to answer
because the situation is so complex. It's like saying tell me all
about yourself and you are an older person and you can't tell
someone all about yourself in two or three sentences. Nor
could I tell you in five minutes why I came to this decision. I
think it has been building up over, I could say fourteen years
or I could say it took fifty-three years to come to such a
decision because no decision is based on just the moment. It
is a culmination of many different experiences and
observances. I have always believed in public schools. I was
educated in public schools.

MR. FOORE: Was your husband?

MRS. MANSOUR: Yes. And if I had a choice, with
expenses paid, I would not put my children in a private
school. I have always preferred public schools, as have so
many of my neighbors, yet they reluctantly have withdrawn
their children from public schools. And they did so while my
husband and I continued to send our children to public
schools. And the private schools were very expensive; many
of the mothers had to go to work, saying "I must put my

children in private school." So, that gives a general picture of the school situation.

I know public school teachers and I know students in the public schools and I think they are some of the finest people I have ever met. My husband substituted in the public schools when he could get a job. He was considered unqualified to teach full-time in the public schools.

MR. FOORE: Why was that?

MRS. MANSOUR: He did not have three hours of education courses.

MR. FOORE: So your husband was not able to get a full-time position?

MRS. MANSOUR: He would get what they call a temporary position, filling in when someone was sick. But he was very seldom called to teach French or German, his subjects. He was called to the gym once, and of course it was always a joke because he was not much of a gym teacher.

MR. FOORE: Can you tell us anything else about the schools that may have led to your decision?

MRS. MANSOUR: I always felt that my job was to send a good citizen to school, a citizen who is ready to learn. At that point I felt my job, in a way, was over. I never even helped with homework; that was each child's responsibility. And I don't believe in teaching a child to read before he goes to school because I have seen too many teachers suffer from children who already know how to read. And yet, Paul and Matthew, my two youngest, were not taught to read, so I attempted to teach them myself. I had to set about reinteresting them in reading. One of the ways I did this was through cooking, by having them read a recipe. As for math, again, they were being taught very little. So we would take a field trip to the bank, I would show the children how to withdraw money, and then we would come home and I would have Matthew subtract that amount from what we had in the bank. Normally, I could not get Matthew to subtract anything, but the personal aspect of this made subtracting far more interesting to him.

MR. MOORE: Yet your older children seem well-educated, and they went through the public schools.

MRS. MANSOUR: Well, let me put it this way. The point at which each of my children began to have great difficulty in school was always earlier and earlier as the schools began to change for the worse. When Paul entered kindergarten he did rather well. They had one of the old-time teachers, as we call them. By the time first grade came around, which is an extremely important year for a child, he hardly knew his name by the end of six weeks, let alone how to do anything else. There were so many changes, from teachers to teaching methods, that he just didn't care. And this became progressively worse. I spent the next three years unconfusing him, trying to undo what had been done. By the third grade he neither wanted to read, had no desire to read, and had lost all interest in school. This was the same pattern that had occurred with my oldest son, but it did not materialize until high-school. So by the time Paul came along I saw all the signs, and was able to attack it at the beginning.

MR. FOORE: What do you mean by an old time teacher?

MRS. MANSOUR: The teachers who have been teaching for years and years, who often know the oldest child, in, say a family of eight, and is still teaching when the youngest enters kindergarten. I realize that just because they have been in the system for 40 years doesn't necessarily make one a good teacher, but I do think this particular kindergarten teacher was outstanding. I didn't go along with a lot of her views, but a lot of her views were things she didn't go along with either but were ideas that had been forced upon her. And that gets to the heart of the matter. It is the system that was breaking down; the individuals were not at fault. The individual teachers themselves did not know what was going on, could not put their finger on the problem of what was wrong. Why can't we do better? Why can't we improve the schools? It became increasingly difficult to do anything with the public schools.

I don't think it is just a school problem, you see. I think the schools are only a reflection of the homes. The school could not do the job that the home was failing to do. You can't send a child to school who has not been trained at home first. The teacher cannot take that responsibility and should not take that responsibility. It's unfair to the teacher.

MR. FOORE: Thank you. No more questions.

And so the court-case continued, with cross-examination of our mother, with testimony from Melanie, and with testimony from the two of us. A painful procedure, we both were brought to tears on different occasions, pummeled by the prosecutor. Why had we insisted on testifying, when we had been given the option of talking to the judge in his chambers? Two immature fourteen-olds were no match for a man on a mission who was convinced he was saving us from some terrible fate. Though some of our comments were spot on, we thought, and some downright funny, as the following exchanges show:

> MR. FOORE: When you were in your foster home, did you go to school?
>
> MARYAM: No
>
> MR. FOORE: Why not?
>
> MARYAM: Because the whole court case was the issue of going to school or not. It seems to me we should have been able to stay at home until it was decided by the Court whether or not we would have had to go to school.

And this bit later on, under cross-examination:

> MR. NUSSELL: Let me ask you why it was that you didn't go to the psychiatric evaluation that was ordered.
>
> MARYAM: Because I don't think there was any evidence that I was in any way mentally retarded or anything.

Finally, we came to closing arguments, and the judge's decision.

> THE COURT: The Court will indicate that the Court does in fact retain jurisdiction of this matter through disposition. Shelter care will continue. The Court will order psychological and psychiatric exams for the children for whom there have not been any yet—Michele and Maryam—and of Mrs. Mansour. The examinations will take place at Children's Hospital. The finding of neglect is not necessarily the be all to end all; there is yet the determination as to how the future of the children will be impacted in terms of who

has custody, whether it be the mother under direction or whether it be some other persons.

The children will be required, pending the disposition, to be placed in public schools.

The Court would propose to set February 24th for the disposition date. Please consult your calendars.

MR. NUSSELL: That's agreeable with the Government, Your Honor.

MR. FOORE: That is agreeable to the defense.

THE COURT: Very well. We'll meet at 10:00 am on that date.

Oh, God. This was horrible. We had begged to be allowed to stay with our mother until the final trial, but to no avail. And now we had to return to the foster home, with a looming two months ahead of us before the next trial and any hope of release.

CHAPTER 9

HOPE SPRINGS ETERNAL

When our mother realized that our sojourn in foster care was not going to end as soon as we had all anticipated, she made sure to furnish us with stationery and stamps and encouraged us to write. The following letter was written by Matthew. It certainly proves her point that a public-school education was not doing him much good, but boy, it does make for an entertaining read. The letter is transcribed below.

Dear
Mother Mansoor,

Me and Paul miss you like heak!
But like you say, we go by the
ruls. We got some teness-shoues
and pants tsherts. ☐☐☐☐☐. like it says:
Sky writeers ar notoriouls. bad spellers.
Just like me \|\|\| call me: Oh\|\|
the twins called and were not
supost too. the were calling from
a pay phone! at best the were
not cult.

Love
youe son
Matt

Dear

Mother Mansour,

Me and Paul miss you like heak!

But like you say, we go by the rules. We got some teness-shoues and pants & sherts. like it says "sky writeers ar notoriouls bad spellers. Just like <u>me</u>!!!! call me: Oh!! the twins called and were not supost <u>too</u>. they were calling from a pay <u>fohone!</u> At lest the were not cult.

Love,

your son

Matt

Here's a letter from Paul, (misspellings included)

Dear Mother, Melanie, and Riley,

We got lost when we were leaving Washington 'cause Mr. Flackmaster [foster father] made a wrong turn and couldn't get back to were we were befor. It took awile before we got on our way. Mr. Flackmaster wants me to tell you that he thought it was very nice of you to have that food and not to worry about us.

I just remembered that we left our <u>bibles</u>! Try to visit us as soon as you can. Bring us some of our clothes like some winter coats not those long things with weird buttens and hoods. But like that gray one that I think belonged to the Seinholds. Also bring me my tennis shoes, socks, ect. ect. ect.

And also our <u>bibles</u>!

Mr. Flackmaster told Mrs. Flackmaster what you said about the foods we eat and so on. He also said that he thought it wasn't very nice that Mr. Nussell [D.A.] wanted to rush us out and barely say goodby. Mr. Flackmaster is being really nice to us and talks to us a lot.

Love,

Paul

PS. I'm really mad I <u>forgot</u> our <u>bibles</u>! mabey you could mail them to us

We twins were constantly thinking about how to return home. Our second escape came in mid-January. Several letters give some of the details of that adventure.

Dear Paul & Matthew,

Boy, have we got news for you! Maryam and I ran home! On Saturday. We walked halfway and took a bus the rest. It was an 11th & E bus which brought us right into Georgetown. When we got to the house, Mrs. Vood and Mrs. Vyre [realtors] were just coming in. They were coming to hold a housesale! Beds and all. Everything for sale. Anyway, Mother, Melanie and Riley were packing. They were getting ready to move to the Harrington Hotel. They had also packed bags for us four to be delivered later by some one.

Well, we went out to dinner at Darnell Hall [Georgetown University dining hall] and then got to spend the night at home. The next day we had to get out by 1:00 so the ladies could hold the housesale. So we went to the Harrington and booked two rooms. We did a little shopping then came back to the Hotel to eat dinner of bread and cheese. But before we could start two policemen came to pick us up. So we had to go. We spent that night at the receiving home, which is pretty bad...

We just have to think of the end of all this when we can all be together in Paradise. I can hardly wait! Maybe we'll see you on Friday. So stay put 'till then.

Love,

Michele

And from our mother:

Sunday, January 11

Dear Paul,

Well, things are happening! Guess where we are?—at the Harrington Hotel!

We moved out of the house this afternoon—and took a bus with all our luggage downtown. And guess who was with us? The girls—M & M!! Yesterday I heard Melanie give out a loud cry—who should come running in the door—but the twins! Mrs. Vood [realtor] came up about the same time and couldn't believe her eyes. They decided on the spur of the moment to walk home! They walked 13 miles then saw a bus. Were we surprised!!

Now, don't you go getting any ideas.

We have given you the order not to attend school--but don't attempt to walk home! The girls are closer—but it was marvelous they made it. We stayed up very late working— but—we put the girls to bed early—they were tired!

Mrs. Vood had a "house sale" today—she sold lots of things to lots of people. Even the piano!!

Many neighbors came, she said, when she called from her home to the hotel. The police came by while she was having the sale demanding to know where the "teen-agers" were, but she didn't tell them.

We came down to the hotel and got two nice rooms. How we missed you boys.

We went and bought the girls some clothes. They were so happy. They have new coats. We had lunch at the Harrington. Then just as we were settled down this evening to eat our cheese and fruit in our room—there was a door knock—and two big policemen came in demanding the girls. They had to go and we went down the elevator together and saw them to the car. They got in the same kind of car that took me. One policeman, the black one, was very nice. The girls remembered meeting him before—and witnessing to him. He just called me and told me where they are. Tomorrow they will be in court.

They were glad to get Jehovah's message not to go to school. The school bus broke down once—and once they missed it.

How are you and Matthew? Write us still to the home address. Our realtor will bring it to us.

We have two bags—for you and Matthew—full of a few things. Can you ask your foster father to get you a Bible at a Kingdom Hall near-by? I'm sure there is one somewhere out there.

We hope all is going well with you and Matthew. It is an interesting experience and Daddy (and JEHOVAH) both are proud of you. To obey Jehovah is to obey your heavenly and earthly father. Both.

When we do what he wants us to do—he gives us many blessings. You do need your Bibles—they are in the packages we are sending. But you could try and get one at a Kingdom Hall.

We are going to court and they may not let us write you too often just to see if you believe in your stand for JEHOVAH without your Mother and Sister & Brother telling you. Write us at our home address.

Love,

Mother

The following letter details the consequences of that escape to home. First, a little background to the letter:

Around the age of 13, I had experienced a grand-mal seizure early one morning when I had awakened around 5:00 a.m. to help Paul deliver newspapers. I passed out, and when I awoke, did not remember anything that had happened immediately prior to the seizure. A subsequent visit to our family doctor left our mother reassured when he recommended just making sure I got plenty of protein in the diet, go easy on sugar, and be careful in early mornings when blood sugar is low. Following these guidelines appeared to work, and that was the only seizure I ever had while at home. However, once we were sent to foster care it became a different matter-

January 12, 1976

Dear Everyone,

I think I'll explain everything from when we left you.

When we got in the police car I suddenly realized that there was a glass wall dividing us from the front seat. I started crying. I couldn't help it. I guess after being taken away and then that. Anyway the policeman was real nice and he stopped the car and let us get up front. He took us to the Youth Division on Rhode Island Ave. where we saw the black policeman who was also there to get us. We went to his office (the black one's) and sat about an hour and a half while he typed up forms. Meanwhile he was telling us that he prayed to Jehovah (and went to church, didn't drink or smoke) but that he didn't think Jehovah heard or answered him. I told him maybe it was because he was working with this government. After that we were taken to the Receiving Home. It's pretty bad. They checked all our baggage downstairs. We could only bring our coats up. Then we went to the second floor where we saw a black lady who asked us our name, age and religion. I don't know why they wanted to know that?! Well, she put us in a room (cell?) with two beds and a little cabinet. There was no extra room. She gave us two gowns, things, rather to sleep in. Oh, guess what? They turn the lights on and off with a key! We can not do it ourselves! So we went to bed and they locked the door.

The next morning we were waken up about 6:00. Maryam started shaking and I got a little nervous. And believe it or not she had a seizure! I yelled for help, but I guess not very loudly no one came. I just sat on the bed and held her arms like Mother did. Her tongue was moving around but people had said that there was no danger of swallowing it so I didn't worry. I knew it would pass, so I just sat there until it was over. Well, that was not the end of the problem. She did not remember a thing about what had happened. I had to tell her that we came home, we had seen you, bought some clothes, etc. She didn't remember even then, at first, but after a while it all came back. Then we had breakfast, which is what all those places serve, scrambled eggs, toast and sausage and milk. They also had a banana, which we ate. As well as some toast and a little milk.

After that we waited until about 8:30 and then six of us girls (there were 8 altogether—2 were white) went downstairs. And, for the first time in my life I was handcuffed. Maryam, me and 1 other girl together, and the 3 others together. We had to make sure we had all our luggage and they had a hard time finding it. We, of course, forgot a bag— the one with the food. We didn't realize it 'till we were already at the court. We went to the building where our hearing was, but not to the same waiting room. We went to the back and were put in a room with the other girls. They kept the door locked. After a while we were called out, and we talked to Mr. Foore [A.L.'s court appointed lawyer] through bars. He said he'd try to be at the hearing but didn't know if he could. He also wondered if you were here. Well, we didn't know if you even knew there was a hearing. Did you? You were supposed to. Then we went back to the cell and waited awhile longer. Next we were called to our hearing and were handcuffed to [go to] the room. The same place where our other hearings were. Another hearing was going on but Mr. Nussell [District Attorney] was already there. Wouldn't you know it! Before we went in though, two men, lawyers, one for each of us wanted to know if we'd be willing to come out here [to the foster home]. We said yes. In the hearing, which was very short, Mr. Nussell requested we be put back here and that was that. Anyway, then they took us to Nussell's office where we waited quite awhile. Meantime, Mr. Foore had a talk with us explaining what will prob. happen [if we continued to refuse to go to school]. We may get sent to an institution where you are forced to go to school, you may be sent to jail, etc. He's really upset at the whole case. He was trying to contact you all.

Then we went to lunch and after that there was a big talk about what to do. Mr. Foore had contacted you and talked a long time and when he hung up I heard a big "God!". They finally arranged for us to come to the Freedon's until Friday when there will be another hearing about the letter you sent us. All your letters we get from now on are under a subpoena to be kept until then so they can see them. To tell the truth, I would rather be out here than in the R.H. or someplace. I'm beginning to think that we should not have come home because we might have been able to stay here for awhile without going to school. I suppose I'm getting scared and I just have to think of the larger picture. If I didn't I'd go crazy. It's going to be so great in the end if we all do the right thing!

I don't know what's going to happen on Friday. We are under a C. Order to go to school 'till then which we are not going to do. That's what the whole court case is about!

We just have to trust in JEHOVAH.

Love, Michele

Here's a letter detailing the foster parents' perspective after we twins escaped their care, and left for home:

Jan. 18, 1976

Dear Melanie,

This morning I was kind of upset and crying a lot. I guess I should be happy that I'm here and not in Laurel, Maryland in one of those homes but since Mother is willing to fill out that paper or send us to school, there's no reason for us to be here. I wonder if I'll be able to endure it?!!

How are your plans about Israel coming? I saw an article in todays newspaper and thought you all might like to see it. I wish we could be with you now. Is there anyway we can get back together sooner? Didn't Riley say something about getting our own Jewish lawyer?! It doesn't seem to me like any of those people at court Friday were on our side. They all seemed against us and it didn't look like they were doing much to get us back together. Oh, well!

We went with Mr. Freedon [foster father] today to "Hardees"—a hamburger place—and brought our lunch home. On the way back he told us his side of the story of what happened last Saturday. He said he came back with some lunch—2 cheeseburgers, milkshakes and french-fries—for us and not finding us home put the milkshakes in the refrigerator and the other things in the oven and left us a note. (He thought we were with Mrs. Thwaite [a neighbor]). Then, coming back at 5 o'clock and finding everything untouched, he went over to the Thwaites (thinking we just spent the whole day there). But she didn't know where we were so he came back and looked for our address, intending to drive there just to see if we were allright. But he couldn't find it so then went to a neighbor who'd had foster children and got a number to call in Washington. It was Saturday night though, so nobody answered. Finally he had to call the police (he didn't want to—other people said he should) but then, when they came and started making a record he told them not to do it because he didn't want our names on the record (We've been on it enough times, though!). So they left. Then when Mrs. Freedon came back at one A.M. she found our address and he said he was going to drive to Washington but she didn't want him there at that time of the night. So she called an agent and he said to call the police. So they came back and I guess contacted D.C. police. But we had the whole day with you so that was pretty good. Anyway, I knew you wondered what had happened so I've written you as soon as I found out.

Yesterday we went to Mrs. Thwaites to borrow some yeast. Of course, we stayed quite a while and in the meantime had a doughnut and coke and two slices of homemade toast! She mentioned ice-skating again and said they had some skates we could use. Mr. Thwaite said the ice was really smooth because there was no snow or rain, just cold weather, and that it was great for skating. I don't know if I want to go skating though. It might be kind of depressing, but then again it could be fun. The pond should be freezing soon. It's been 12 today and is supposed to be near 30 tomorrow. It was quite cold yesterday too.

It's funny, though. I don't really want cold weather or snow out here. I guess it's because we can't stay out as long then and it gets awfully cramped in this house. This winter seems to be passing away. It's probably because I push the days until we see you. I don't really live them. (Do you understand that?)

Love,

Maryam

Now regarding those "plans about Israel" mentioned in that last letter. After being kicked out of Jehovah's Witnesses, our mother felt a bit rootless, religion-wise. She had learned a lot about the Bible through her studies with the Witnesses, reading both Hebrew and Christian-Greek testaments thoroughly (*not* to

be called "Old" and "New" testaments according to the
Witnesses. Both, the Witnesses teach, are relevant to
understanding God's plan for mankind, and one does not negate
the other). Anyway, she apparently felt that since she could not
be a Witness, the closest thing that made sense was Judaism. And,
since we currently had no home—why not emigrate to Israel?! As
in all her undertakings, she dove right in. But more on those
adventures later.

CHAPTER 10

FINAL VERDICT

And so began a period of endurance in foster care. We enrolled in school, and oh, how we hated getting on that school bus every day. Having been used to the freedom of walking to school, the experience of getting on that bus as two shy and awkward fourteen-year-olds was somehow doubly painful. We made no friends. Home and family was where our hearts were and we constantly wrote letters—to the boys, our mother, Riley and Melanie. Basically, we were just waiting for the February 24th trial date, on which we had set our hopes.

By now our mother realized she was not going to be supported in the courts by Jehovah's Witnesses, and that standing on principle meant she may never see her children again. She decided to agree to return us to school.

February 24th arrived. We children were brought to the D.C. court by our social workers, and were overjoyed when we saw our family. In the court room was the usual cast of characters, as well as four psychologists or psychiatrists. Much of the testimony has been cut for brevity.

MR. NUSSELL: Your Honor, we are here this morning for a disposition hearing, the Court having found the four children neglected at a prior hearing at the conclusion of the trial.

Your Honor, I took the liberty of subpoenaing the psychologists and psychiatrists who participated in the evaluation of the children.

What I had hoped we could do this morning was perhaps something in the nature of a plenary nature, at which time each of those persons could offer to the Court the basis of their recommendations.

THE COURT: Very well. Perhaps the persons could be seated in the jury box. There is simply no room in chambers to accommodate everyone

MR. NUSSELL: That would be fine. Those of you from the Children's Hospital, and Mrs. Fergman, would you please be seated in the jury box?

MR. NUSSELL: Your Honor, initially, I'm asking that the Court commit the four children to the Social Rehabilitation Administration for two years. I'm asking that during this commitment period that Mrs. Mansour participate in a program of psychotherapy. I'm asking for a full Court review in one year. Now, perhaps most useful, if I could begin and ask the three psychologists who saw the children to give to the Court an indication of what their examinations revealed.

MRS. FERGMAN: At this point, I would ask that the children wait outside the Courtroom until we've heard from the psychologists.

THE COURT: Very well, the children will be excluded.

We four younger ones are escorted out and put in a room to await the outcome of the hearing.

MR. NUSSELL: Thank you, Your Honor. I would like to begin with Dr. Maleita. Please indicate who you saw, and the essence of these evaluations.

DR. MALEITA: I saw Michele. She's of at least a bright normal intelligence. I feel like she's physically a normal teenager. I think that there's some underlying feelings that she would like to escape the situation and more or less live a normal life.

As far as recommendations go, I think Michele would profit from being in a situation where there is little conflict. And I feel that Michele has a lot of potential to be a very successful human being.

MR. NUSSELL: Dr. Leymour, if I may.

DR. LEYMOUR: Yes. I saw Matthew, who is a very intelligent, very bright delightful young man. He seems to have developed before his age a lot of adult defenses, which are causing him a great deal of anxiety. He seems to be afraid to really let himself into personal social relationships with a great deal of freedom and emotional wants. He is a creative child, wants to relate, but is somehow fearful of letting himself go with other people.

MR. NUSSELL: All right. Dr. Shagenau

DR. SHAGENAU: I saw both Paul and Maryam, and I saw Paul first. He's also very bright. He may be of very superior intelligence. He took a very strong pro-family stance and stated very definitely that he wanted to go home. He did not like the foster placement.

I felt he was a rather anxious boy and would certainly benefit from being in an environment where he would be provided with the comfort and security kind of thing. All in all, I felt that he was a fairly normal child.

The other child I saw was Maryam. And Maryam also appears to be a very bright child. She was rather articulate. I was concerned with several things with Maryam, however.

She was extremely anxious. I felt the family, perhaps, was a source of distress. She seems to have a strong need for some kind of situation where she can get some kind of a handle on her anxiety and calm down, feel more secure, feel better about herself.

THE COURT: Thank you. We'll go to Dr. Dostell now.

DR. DOSTELL: I saw Mrs. Mansour for approximately two hours in the course of a clinical interview. And Mrs. Mansour was prompt, cooperative and quite helpful in the way of providing information which I think has helped me in understanding better the kind of stresses which she had been subject to over the last two years. My concern about Mrs. Mansour is in two areas. One, the question of depression. And the other, the question as to what extent her actions could be seen as reflecting a psychotic process. That is a process in which a person is unable to deal rationally with reality. My sense was that with regard to the depression, that Mrs. Mansour was making progress in coping with the more severe depression that she had felt previously, after her husband died. With regard to the question of psychosis, I do not believe that Mrs. Mansour is psychotic. It's a difficult kind of distinction to make in view of some of the idiosyncratic ideas held by the family. But to the extent to which some of her feelings of persecution are supported by independent information about concerns of relatives and neighbors, I do not feel that represents a kind of paranoid delusion. With regard to her religious notions, to the extent they are shared by a large social reference group, the Jehovah's Witness faith, that cannot be classified as delusional.

My recommendation with regard to Mrs. Mansour is that I feel she can benefit from psychiatric counseling. There is also a possibility that she could benefit from treatment with medication, although I will not make a definite commitment to that plan at this point.

THE COURT: Mr. Nussell?

MR. NUSSELL: Thank you, your Honor. I would like to ask each of you your judgment of the situation.

DR. LEYMOUR: Well, I feel that Matthew needs to be circled in a position for some period of time in which he can become freer to express some of the emotions and concerns that he would like to which are more appropriate for his age level.

THE COURT: All right.

DR. MALEITA: I think that Michele needs a place where she can feel free to do whatever she wants to do. I feel that she should be returned to the foster home at this time.

DR. SHAGENAU: As far as Maryam is concerned, I don't think that she should return home at this time. Paul should be allowed to be in a situation where he can loosen up a little bit, if you will, to do the kind of things that he wants to do and really be in an environment where he can come to terms with a lot of his feelings. I would not send him home.

THE COURT: Thank you.

MR. NUSSELL: Your Honor, I would like to explore one other matter with the doctors.

THE COURT: Yes.

MR. NUSSELL: Should the court follow this recommendation and continue with the children in foster homes, what kind of recommendations do you have in terms of intra-family contact, visitation, communication?

DR. LEYMOUR: Well, to the extent that contact is going to be very, very upsetting to the children in terms of keeping them in total conflict with what they are feeling and what parents may be asking them to do, it could be detrimental to their development during this period of separation.

MR. NUSSELL: Let me ask if all of you can concur?

All the psychiatrists nod their heads.

THE COURT: Mrs. Mansour?

MRS. MANSOUR: I have no questions

THE COURT: Do you have any statement which you wish to make at this time?

MRS. MANSOUR: I would indeed.

THE COURT: All right. You may remain seated where you are

MRS. MANSOUR: Judge Harvey, I am a mother of eight children and a widow. I appear before you today as was done in Solomon's Court, to plead my case. I move that the Court declare a mistrial in this case for the following reasons.

One: That the First, Fifth, Sixth, Eighth, Ninth, Thirteenth and Fourteenth Amendments to the Constitution of the United States were violated.

Two: That I was prosecuted under Title 16 but was guilty of violating Title 31 of the DC. Code.

Your Honor, I rest my case.

THE COURT: Mrs. Mansour, the Court has heard you, but the Court has to say that in any proffer which one makes to the Court that constitutional rights have been violated, it is necessary that the Court be told how it is applicable in the particular case.

MRS. MANSOUR: I do have more to present. Judge Harvey, may my son read?

THE COURT: Very well, he can make a statement as a witness in your behalf.

MRS. MANSOUR: Thank you

RILEY: In the Court case concerning Michele Mansour, Maryam Mansour, Paul Mansour and Matthew Mansour, constitutional errors were committed.

The First Amendment rights of the aforementioned defendants were violated on the following grounds: The Superior Court of the District of Columbia Family and

Neglect Branch, by Court order, prevented the free exercise of religion.

The Fifth Amendment rights of the aforementioned defendants were violated on the following grounds: That the five defendants were compelled to be witnesses against themselves.

The Sixth Amendment rights of the aforementioned defendants were violated on the following grounds: That the defendants were not given a "public trial by an impartial jury of the state".

The Eighth Amendment rights of the aforementioned defendants were violated on the following grounds: That cruel and unusual punishment was inflicted on the four minor defendants in that they were placed in foster homes outside the District of Columbia and that such placement is unusual because in no other state of the union are children taken out of the local Court's jurisdiction.

The Ninth Amendment on the following grounds: The defendant Annie Laurie Mansour and the four minors were treated and handled legally as guilty and not treated and handled legally as innocent until proven guilty.

The Thirteenth Amendment rights of the aforementioned defendants were violated on the following grounds: That the statute under which the defendants were convicted is unconstitutional.

The Fourteenth Amendment rights of the aforementioned defendants were violated on the following grounds: The defendants were tried and convicted under the law that prohibits their free exercise of religion as provided under the First Amendment.

THE COURT: Thank you. Mr. Nussell, do you wish to make any response?

MR. NUSSELL: Your Honor, I think I simply request the court to deny the motion for a mistrial, deny the grounds as cited by Mr. Mansour are applicable and are fairly erroneous.

THE COURT: The Court, in fact, does deny the mistrial. No one has been found guilty. What has been found is that the minor respondents in this case were the subject of neglect.

MRS. MANSOUR: Judge Harvey, may I ask you?

THE COURT: Yes.

MRS. MANSOUR: It is incredible to me that I have heard what I heard this morning. My entire experience from the very beginning of this case has been incredible. I have dealt with lies. I have dealt with people who seem in their positions not to tell the truth. I have felt all along if I could have brought my children to you and I had had all the people who were involved in this in one room together and we could have talked this thing out very briefly, the entire matter would have been resolved. I still feel that.

It is inconceivable to me what is going on here, as much as I enjoyed hearing these people this morning. I would not say that they were all wrong about my children. I have learned something from you all. No parent knows exactly how to raise a child. I have done the best I could. And of course after the death of my husband I may have behaved somewhat erratically. But if a widow behaves somewhat erratically after her husband's death, is it necessarily wrong? Does it justify taking my children from me? I feel sure that everyone here has a part of the truth. But the whole truth has not come out in the Courtroom. As you know, I'm not really a lawyer. But I have understood, and my family and I have been very disturbed by what we have seen go on. There is no one in here who really would tear this family apart if all the truth were put into the Courtroom.

I even thought Mr. Nussell's idea of having everyone gather around a table is the right idea. I know it can be resolved. Because we are going down a very dangerous road by removing my children from me for no real reason. And when the whole truth is not known, very dangerous things occur.

THE COURT: What do you contend is the truth?

MRS. MANSOUR: The truth is that I am raising my family to the best of my ability. I am a Jehovah's Witness. I do believe that Jehovah is God. I do read the scriptures. The Bible has the truth.

And though we have had this quarrel with the Jehovah's Witnesses, it is not so deep that it couldn't be solved. For I feel that all people are after the truth. And I don't think any one religious body really has all the truth. The truth is here in this Courtroom if all these people would step out of their positions and come in and listen to it.

But we're each going our separate ways. It's like the story of the blind men touching an elephant—one man touches the tail and claims it's a rope, another touches a leg and claims it's a tree, the next one touches an ear and thinks it's a fan. Each thought he was right based on his own experience, but because they didn't have the whole picture they were all wrong.

And in this case these children should not be taken from me. I beg you, do not take my children.

THE COURT: Mrs. Mansour, what has been presented earlier alludes heavily toward your having been charged with a crime. The fact is you were not being prosecuted for anything.

MRS. MANSOUR: I have one other statement to make, Your Honor.

THE COURT: Very well.

MRS. MANSOUR: As required by Title 31, Section 201 of the DC.Code, I will put my children in the city schools of the District of Columbia. I give you my word on this.

THE COURT: Well, the Court hears you and that of course is a step in the right direction. But other things now have to be taken into consideration. And the Court does not feel that you are in a position to provide the emotional background and support and under-girding that is necessary with respect to all four of these children.

MRS. MANSOUR: May I make one more statement?

I do not understand how any decision can be rendered by people who do not know the situation. You are total strangers to me and my family. Do I see anybody in this Courtroom who speaks in my defense? Is there anyone in here who has known me 30 or 40 years and known my family and my husband from the College of Charleston, South Carolina, and Washington, from Berlin, from Vienna, from Kentucky? With what I have put up with for the past six weeks from people who are supposed to have my children's welfare in mind, if I am getting emotional, Judge Harvey, I have earned the right to be emotional

THE COURT: Of course. Of course.

MRS. MANSOUR: Jehovah has given me the right to be emotional after what I have put up with from people who do not know the situation, who have done everything to solve a family situation where there was no problem. I know Paul, I know him well. And I know Michele's problems. I have not been a perfect mother in some areas, I admit that. I spent 27 years raising a family of eight children, and then my husband died. And it is not easy being a widow, but I have grown and learned since then. And my children have helped bring me through an extremely trying time in my life.

It is incredible to me that anyone, that anyone would rule against my family after what I have been through. I realize that I made errors. But I plead with you that my children be returned to me, Judge Harvey, and I will put them in school. I have looked up the schools I would like them to go to. I am now living in the heart of town and I want to put my children in the city schools. I have talked to the principals of Ross and Stevens schools. There are so many things that I want to show my children in that area of D.C, and I am particularly interested in the Stevens School because I hear there are so many students from all over the world attending there.

THE COURT: The Court's judgement remains the same with one exception. The exparte review will occur in approximately 90 days, rather than six months.

MR. NUSSELL: Thank you, Your Honor.

May I suggest, Your Honor, that there be a moratorium on visits for one month and limited and supervised visits thereafter. And may I suggest as to the mail, that Mrs. Mansour be limited to one letter per week and that no letters at all be permitted from either Riley or Melanie Mansour. As I understand it, each of these three family members have been sending letters just about every day, which deluges the children with 21 or so letters a week.

THE COURT: Very well.

We children are brought back into the courtroom to hear the verdict.

THE COURT: Young ladies and gentlemen, the purpose of this hearing was to make a determination of what should be done with respect to your care and custody, having previously determined, as the Court advised you, that a kind of neglect had occurred in that you were not being sent to the public schools or, in the alternative, being offered education which was equivalent to that offered in the public schools.

We have heard a great many things this morning. The decision which the Court has made is that you will continue under commitment to the Social Rehabilitation Administration. And that there will be a review in approximately 90 days, which will not require the presence of all parties.

Within that period of time, the Court for the first month will prohibit any visits on the part of your older sister and your older brother and your mother. And thereafter, visits will be arranged at the discretion of the Department of Human Resources. There will be a moratorium on the letters written to you by your mother to the extent that they will be restricted to twice weekly. And they will be subject to monitoring by the Department of Human Resources.

The Court has considered that as a result of the information which has come through from the persons who interviewed you and made evaluations, that all of you are entitled to a certain kind of freedom to think matters through and be given a certain independence of thought, which, in some case, you all want.

The Court is in no way interfering with your religious beliefs and the Court is not saying you should not hold to whatever your religious beliefs are. The Court has no criticism of you nor any other persons who adhere to the belief of Jehovah's Witnesses.

But the Court has determined that in the process of exercising that belief, those persons have in fact violated the law and that your religion does not compel a violation of the law.

When a determination of neglect has been made, then a great many other factors entered into the decisions at to what shall be done. And those other factors are such things as to what is determined on the basis of your interviews.

Thus, in addition to the fact of your continued commitment, the Court is requiring that Maryam enter into

a program of psychotherapy. That Mrs. Mansour participate
in a program of psychotherapy. That Maryam has the need
of some medical attention and will be given a neurological
exam. The Court is also requiring that your brother Riley
undergo a psychiatric evaluation, as we look at a long-range
program for your final return to your home.

The Court is informed and already was of the
opinion that all of you have tremendous potential and
possibilities. That all of you are bright and intelligent and
have great capacity for learning, for growth, for
development. And it is the Court's judgment that under the
program which we are attempting to provide for you, you
will have the best possibility to develop those potential
talents that you have.

Thereupon the proceedings were concluded at 12:40
p.m.

We could not believe it. Our mother had finally agreed to
send us to school. She had even researched the public schools in
downtown D.C. where she was now living. What did these
people want? Well, as subjects of Jehovah's Kingdom we were not
obligated to obey these laws, were we? Heck no! And so—we
fled.

CHAPTER 11

IMPRISONMENT

We have no idea why we were not more closely watched, but at the conclusion of the trial all seven of us simply walked out of the court building. Without a plan in our heads, we just wanted to somehow escape. A block or two from the courthouse what should we come across but a bright-red, double-decker British tour-bus sitting empty by the side of the road. We all clambered aboard; hoping it would take off, perhaps? But as we sat there and no driver materialized, we began to feel like sitting ducks. So down and out we all go, sneaking into a nearby church for another temporary hiding place. We still worried they might find us; we were just blocks from the courthouse. What now? "I know," our mother said, "Let's get to the bus station. We'll go to New York." She sent Melanie ahead to buy the tickets. Ten minutes felt like an hour as we huddled inside the church, waiting. Paul peeked out the door checking for any policemen. When he reported that he did not see any, we gingerly emerged from the building and walked the two blocks to the bus station, keeping an eye out for police. As we drew close, we saw Melanie coming from the ticket office, tickets waving in her hand. We shouted and ran towards her. Simultaneously we heard sirens and turned around, anxiously looking to see where the police cars were coming from. But we were too late. One car pulled up between us and Melanie, and another behind us. We were surrounded by four cops as they jumped from the cars and grabbed each of the four children.

We were not about to go down without a battle, though. Oh no, we refused to go quietly. We fought and resisted arrest as best we could, jumping out the far side of the cop car the minute they put us in the other. This happened several times until they decided to send in a paddy wagon. Finally, at one point, cops and detectives were holding us by the arms and legs, attempting to throw us in the paddy wagon. Had we not been so concerned about messing up their slacks we would have kicked harder and escaped the paddy wagon; we are convinced our good manners got the best of us. Eventually all four of us were thrown kicking and screaming into the paddy wagon, joined by none other than the D.A. himself, Mr. Nussell.

Paul's take on the event is shown in this letter:

Feb 24, 1976

Dear Mother,

After we were put in the patty wagon Mr. Nussell got in and we had a rather emotional conversation. We called him a liar and cryed and carried on for awhile. We were taken to a office some place where the twins had been before and we were all starving to and we told the police so and they kind a grinned. Then we went to Mrs. Furman's [social worker] office and the police wouldn't let us ride in the same car because there was a law of some sort that boys and girls can't ride in the same car!!! At Mrs. Furman's office we demanded a decent meal and so they took us to a place right around the corner from the building her office is.

I hope you get things worked out at court and we can get back as soon as possible.

Love,

Paul

And here is Michele's perspective on the incident:

Feb 24, 1976

Dear Mother, Riley, & Melanie,

A few minutes ago we got Mother's phone call. As soon as we knew it was you we ran to the phone and tried to listen in, as, of course, we couldn't talk directly to you. I think Mrs. Freedon [foster mother] thought you'd be very low and was surprised at how "chipper" you sounded. Though you may not have been as happy (whatever) as you sounded. It's too bad we couldn't see you if you came in to Manassas. If you wanted to see Mr. Freedon you'd probably have to come on a week-end because he gets home pretty late from work. We talked to them about what happened with the police and all and they loved it. Mr. Freedon said he should have been there since he's never heard us holler or yell. (He always wants to hear us raise our voices). Boy, he would have heard it then! You know, Mr. Nussell was in the paddy wagon with us and I think he enjoyed the whole episode. I know I did—that was exciting! I'm just mad I didn't struggle harder! That Baptist guy kept showing us scriptures but somehow he bugs me. I think he thinks a "true" christian should always be cool, calm and collected. Well, Jesus wasn't always that and if he wasn't a true christian, who is?

I guess we'll be going to school. I hope it's okay, but it would get pretty boring staying around here all day.

Great news! (or do you already know?) Mrs. Ferman [social worker] isn't on this case anymore! Hurray! It's transferred to Mrs. Feecham (not that she's much better). Mrs. Freedon said you'd talked to her I think, so maybe you know already.

After we were taken to the office on Rhode Island Av. we were starving and asked for food. They offered us candy and potato chips if we had any money. Paul yelled "we want a meal" but they just sort of grinned. So when they took us to Mrs. Ferman's office we asked again and they took us to this restaurant called "Bills"—you'd like it—they serve Beer!— where we got a veal cutlet sandwich, like Ikaros, and a coke. So at least we got something. After that Mrs. Lobel [social worker] wanted to talk to us and we asked her some questions. One was about what Riley had read and she said that was under the "criminal" law, etc. Baloney! We also complained about the Freedons and she said she'd talk to Mrs. Feecham about it. Actually I guess they're alright and I wonder if anywhere else would be better. We're hoping that since it seems kind of permanent now (ugh!) that we could get somewhere with the boys. There must be some larger foster homes! And we started saying how boring it was (with the Freedons) and how exciting living with you was and she said that was funny because in the psychologists reports they said that, though on the surface we wanted to live the way we were living, deep down we wanted a more stable life!

#@**#@?&&@ As if they know. Why can't we say what we feel-deep down. Those guys lied to us, I think. They seemed to believe it would all come out alright but their testimonies defied that. They're in cahoots with Nussell, I'm sure.

What on earth did you guys do after we were taken away? Did people come up to you or anything? We didn't even know if you'd been taken too, or not. It seems that you aren't destined to go to jail, know what I mean? No matter what you do you're usually left alone. So that's good—at least some of us can move around and stuff.

Well, thanks for the call—it was fun even if we didn't talk. I heard you, Mother, did you hear us yell "by"?

Love, and Hastily

Michele

P.S. A Ramada Inn is right across the highway from us and a Holiday Inn real close, too. We could go for a walk and meet in secret!

These letters from us over the next months indicate that some resignation has set in.

February 27, 1976

Dear Riley,

We received a letter from Paul today saying Mother had called them too the evening after the court case. He also said that Mrs. Flackmaster [the boys' foster mother] had told them that Mrs. Feecham [social worker] had called her and said that they would be out there for a whole year, and that if they try to run away or don't go to school, etc., they might have to stay 2 or 3 years or even for good. I believe we may have to stay separated 1 or 2 years but I don't think it's nice of the Flackmasters to scare the boys like that. Paul was telling us at court that they threaten them when they're sick not to be absent more than 2 days or they have to get a note from their doctor, and that Mr. Flackmaster gets mad at them if they don't go. But Paul said other children only bring a note from home if they're out for long, so the Flackmasters probably do that just to scare them. Paul also said that they told them not to cry at school—else it might affect the trial adversely. That makes me mad. I really think they ought to cry (Matthew said he did and got sent to the nurse's office) to show how unhappy they are—which is just what the Flackmasters don't want, I'm sure.

Matthew told us (when we were at court) that his school is the open-classroom type where you can hear the other teachers talking. He said he gets special tutoring in math because everyone else is on division and he's still on his times tables (he doesn't like it).

A young couple who live next door to the Freedon's [foster parents] have a boat which they go fishing in during the summer and they said they might take us. It would be fun if the boys could come too.

Love,
Maryam
March 29, 1976
Dear Riley,

As we told Mother, we thought it would be nice if we could go visit Paul and Matthew. So this morning the social worker was to call and we wanted Mrs. Freedon to ask her if it would be alright for us to see the boys. But she said they only had a minute to talk and what they talked about is that they're trying to put Mother in a mental hospital. As a matter of fact,

Mother was there at the moment and apparently a whole lot of people were discussing what should be done with her.

I hope Mother is alright. Where are you and Melanie now? Or did they let Mother go back to the Tabard Inn? I have a sinking feeling that we won't get back together until Satan is abyssed. That's two years from now and if it is that long, I hope it will pass quickly. Sometimes it seems as if we are just waiting for Armageddon.

Anyway, I'm praying that everything's okay and the only way I'm going to endure it is to laugh at it. Otherwise their "lunatic logic" is going to kill me.

Love,

Maryam

Around this time, the courts not only recommended psychiatric treatment for most of us, but they also recommended medical treatment for me due to my seizures. While our mother was confident in the diagnosis of our family doctor, who felt the issue could be remedied by correct diet and rest, the courts were not. I was sent to a Dr. Anne Fruelein at Georgetown University Medical Center. A neurologist, she wanted to give me more tests, and prescribed phenobarbital. Learning of the side effects, including a drowsiness which would preclude an ability to even ride a bicycle, I refused to take the pills. When our mother learned what the courts were up to, she wrote the following letter:

May 16, 1976

Dear Dr. Freulein:

If you listen to the United States Courts to force testing and medicine on Maryam Mansour, you are making the same mistakes that the Germans made under Hitler when he set himself up as Fuhrer.

Germany's problem under the Nazi's is summed up in one scripture: "Auch lasst euch nicht, Fuhrer nennen, den einer ist euer Fuhrer, der Christus." (Matthaus 23:10- "Neue-Welt-Ubersetgung der Heiligen Schrift")

The Scriptures further add: "Denn Jehova ist unser Richter, Jehova ist unser Satzungsgeber, Jehova ist unser Koneg; er selbst wird uns retten." (Jesaja 33:22)

We also recommend the following Biblical passage—Mark 9:14-29.

Sincerely yours,

Annie Lauire Riley Mansour

F. Riley Mansour

Melanie Mansour

We were battling on all fronts. But our mother continually inspired us to stay strong, as evidenced in the letter below (names have been redacted to protect the guilty).

Dear Paul and Matthew,   May 1 - '76
Maryam and Michele,

I am writing this letter to all of you through Mrs.
_____ (pronounced _____)
Like Mrs. _____, she will be reading this letter
before sending it on to you.
This is an important letter.

First, we want to commend you for your superior
missionary activity. The Times Square Congregation
which we attend here in New York city has been
fully informed about this case and they are in
contact with Bethel headquarters concerning it.
You are residing in the 👁 of the storm and
cannot see (nor can we completely) the whirlwind
of activity and the speeding electrons which sur-
round the nucleus. Happily, many positrons are
forming for Jehovah's name — and to help us!
(I hope you have not forgotten our science
lesson on atomic energy.)   ← electron
positron = positive electron
when an anti-particle meets its   nucleus
anti-partner, the two destroy each   proton
other - releasing 🌟 energy !!!   neutron

Remember: Two ⊖ negatives make a ⊕ positive 🚶x🚶 = ✝

Page 2

Here is an article in the May 1, Watchtower

This shows we have more in common with witnesses in foreign lands than we do in many parts of America. Your father did not like persecution of Jehovah's Witnesses.

Remember Maryam & Michele were taken at night by police →

prisoned from three months to a year because their children have refused to take part in flag ceremonies. They have steadfastly followed the course of the faithful Hebrews mentioned in the third chapter of Daniel. This issue has involved at least one thousand cases. According to the law, children can be taken from their parents if the judges find it advisable. Pregnant mothers have been incarcerated with all sorts of criminal types, and have been forced to leave little ones at home in an effort to stop these mothers from teaching their children God's Word.—Ex. 20:4, 5.

¹⁴ A brother, fifty-seven years of age, was accused of proselytism and was fined $100. A sister nineteen years of age was sentenced to a month in a penitentiary for the same reason. Many have been accused of being involved with the American C.I.A. to stir up hatred against them. Brothers are often arrested for having "illicit meetings," sometimes even being arrested on such charge late at night when everyone in the home is sleeping. Some have been imprisoned for their conscientious objection to military service. Many have suffered beatings or were forced to work long hours in the fields. Three brothers were sentenced to two years in prison for refusing to work on tobacco for reasons of conscience. The government does not permit children of Jehovah's Witnesses to attend meetings for religious instruction. Kingdom Halls have been closed and all types of restrictions have been put on Christian meetings so that newly interested persons and young ones cannot receive instruction in God's Word. Yet still the brothers write: "Jehovah our God is the one in whom we have to trust. Jehovah loves his people tenderly and he shows his power marvelously."

¹³ That this hatred exists in modern times can be seen by the following reports from various parts of the world. The Witnesses in a Spanish-speaking country report: "There is a campaign against us on all fronts, on the radio, over the TV, in the newspapers, in worker centers, at the hospitals, in the streets, in the schools, even block by block. A great number of friends are without jobs. We are as the Israelites in Egypt. We continue encouraging the friends to go on with the good news because no demon or human can stop them." However, the brothers face severe hardships. Parents have been im-

14. In what ways have the Witnesses in one country been put under pressure?

15. What trials and hardships have the brothers had to endure, and how have they been strengthened?

THE WATCHTOWER — MAY 1, 1976

more this!

our school was closed

READ! ←

as you know, I was jailed 30 hours and met many people who were eager to hear the Good News about Jehovah!! →

Seven brothers were imprisoned for some months in this country, but the circuit overseer reported: "They are busy preaching the good news to their fellow prisoners." Arrangements were made for these brothers to be helped with food so that they did not have to suffer unduly during their imprisonment.

Page 3   A note just to Matthew and Paul
→ (Maryam & Michele have their own note)
Here are some questions ?????

1. How is the ░░░░░░░░░░░

2. Do you have a ░░░░░ GARDEN ?

3. Have you caught any 🐸🐸🐸 lately ?

4. How are all the 🧍🧍🧍🧍 ?

5. How is 🏫 $6 \times 2 = 12$?
   $3 \times 3 = 9$
   $5 + 4 = 20$

6. Do you have a 🏘️ you are building ?

7. How is Mr. ░░░░ 🚚 ?

Matthew & Paul: Please write me
and let me know you have
received this letter. (3 pages)

Guess what today is ?   Love,   Mother

⚫ Day!   ← my horse is not good! Paul
in old Kentucky! in the Blue Grass!

P.S. Please greet Mr. & Mrs.

CHAPTER 12

ALIYAH

While we were planning escapes or plotting undercover visits, the three on the home front were also plotting strategies for our release. How to convince the courts that our mother was fit to raise us? Time to get to work on the plans to move to Israel.

After selling our home in D.C., and spending a few nights in the Harrington Hotel, Annie Laurie moved with Riley and Melanie to an old hotel in D.C., The Tabard Inn. She loved living downtown with its hustle and bustle, and restaurants and shopping all within easy walking distance. Foxhall Village seemed suburban and dull by comparison. We received many letters from our mother while she lived at the Tabard Inn, a place she would have loved for us to see and enjoy, but we were never allowed to visit her during that time.

Then Annie Laurie, Riley and Melanie made the decision to move to New York City. This was not an impulsive idea. During the year following our father's death, our mother had discussed with us the idea of relocating to New York. Having been reacquainted with the city after our trip to attend the Jehovah's Witness convention, she thought it would be a good move for the family. We were all thrilled with the idea, though were curious as to how one actually *lived* in a place such as New York City. Due, however, to the government's interference the plan had been placed on hold. Now she decided to move ahead. With the furniture gone, the homestead sold, and a few items of clothing in tow, the three initially lodged in the hotel we had stayed in while attending that convention in 1973—The Iroquois Hotel on West 44th Street just off Fifth Avenue. This would allow easy access to Bethel, the headquarters of Jehovah's Witnesses located in Brooklyn Heights, New York. Annie Laurie still had lingering hope that the Witnesses would come to our defense based on the Biblical principles we were following.

Since a hotel was considered temporary housing, and not up to the Court's standards for us children, during this time she also booked passage for seven on a ship going to Israel.

To get us younger four enthused she sent us many articles, brochures, and photos of Israel, bound in books made of construction paper. And we fell right in line, poring over the brochures and getting excited to think about living on a kibbutz— what an adventure that would be!

But first, there was the matter of the illegal visit she had made to make sure we children were OK. Annie Laurie, accompanied by Melanie, had visited Manassas, Virginia, the location of our foster home. She met our foster parents outside the home, at a hotel nearby, so as not to violate the court order prohibiting visits the first month. But then she made a second visit, just before that month ended. The court transcripts tell the story. The booking to Israel also becomes a bone of contention with the judge.

Mr. Nussell, Mrs. Feecham [social worker] Annie Laurie, Riley and Melanie appear in the courtroom

THE COURT: You may proceed.

MR. NUSSELL: Your Honor, before coming before the Court today, Mrs. Mansour approached me in the hallway and indicated she had made some attempts to obtain the services of an attorney for today and apparently she was not successful in that. And she contacted me by phone yesterday to indicate that she wished the matter to be continued. Perhaps the Court would wish to inquire of Mrs. Mansour along those lines.

THE COURT: Mrs. Mansour?

MRS. MANSOUR: I'm here because I asked for the possibility of a continuance, but I've changed my mind. I'd made arrangements with a shipping company in New York for tickets to Israel. And they ended up having 7 tickets available for sailing on April 23rd, rather than waiting for September, and that is a rare thing. So rather than ask for a continuance I would like to present this evidence that we are going to Israel and this should please the Court because we will have a place for the children. I have been working on this for quite some time- for a change of location for me and my family.

THE COURT: So you are not asking for a continuance? You understand that the matter that is presently before the Court is a show cause hearing?

MRS. MANSOUR: Yes, I do.

THE COURT: Mr. Nussell, you may proceed.

MR. NUSSELL: Thank you. Your Honor, on the 5th day of April 1976 the Court entered an order ordering Mrs. Mansour to appear on today's date at 10:00 to show cause as to why she should not be held in contempt regarding her appearance at the Freedon foster home in Manassas, Virginia. I believe that the Government will show beyond a reasonable doubt that Mrs. Mansour was indeed in direct violation of the order of this Court. I'd like to call Miss Jean Feecham.

Thereupon, Jean Feecham, having been called as a witness for and on behalf of the Government, and having been first duly sworn by the clerk, was examined and testified as follows:

MR. NUSSELL: Miss FEECHAM, during the course of your duties as a social worker in the Department of Social Services, did you have occasion to become involved with the Mansour family?

MISS FEECHAM: Yes. I was assigned as the family social worker approximately five weeks ago.

MR. NUSSELL: At some time during the day or evening of March 24, 1976, did you have a conversation with Mrs. Mansour by telephone?

MISS FEECHAM : Yes, I did.

MR. NUSSELL: Will you explain to the Court how that occurred?

MISS FEECHAM: Yes. I was asked by our after-hours emergency service to call the foster mother. When I did she indicated that Mrs. Mansour and Melanie were in the foster home and I asked her if I could speak with them.

MR. NUSSELL: And during the course of your conversation with Mrs. Mansour did you talk to her in regard to whether or not she had permission to be there?

MISS FEECHAM: Yes, I did

MR. NUSSELL: What was Mrs. Mansour's response to those statements by you?

MISS FEECHAM: Mrs. Mansour replied that her orders were from Jehovah.

MR. NUSSELL: During the course of the call, after you indicated she was in the home without permission, did she indicate she had to leave to comply with the order?

MISS FEECHAM: No, she did not. She remained.

MR. NUSSELL: No other questions.

Cross examination by Mrs. Mansour

MRS. MANSOUR: Miss Feecham, have you spoken to Mrs. Freedon [foster mother] about me and my visits and the children?

MISS FEECHAM: We have had many conversations.

MRS. MANSOUR: Has she indicated to you that she did not want me visiting?

MR. NUSSELL: Objection, Your Honor, that is irrelevant.

THE COURT: Objection sustained. That's beside the point, Mrs. Mansour. The purpose of this hearing is to determine whether you are in contempt of this Court's order.

MRS. MANSOUR: All right. Did Mrs. Freedon ever tell you that we stayed the entire afternoon and she let me talk to the children and seemed to enjoy the visit?

MISS FEECHAM : I inquired how long you were there.

MRS. MANSOUR: I want to ask you if you've ever spoken to Mr. Freedon with regard to this case?

MISS FEECHAM: I talked to Mr. Freedon after talking to you. As you know, you mentioned to Mr. Freedon that he was the person who should request your leaving and that you would not leave unless he requested it. And I understand that as a Jehovah you believe that the male parent should request this. And I asked Mr. Freedon to ask this.

MRS. MANSOUR: As a Jehovah's Witness I asked the head of the house to make the decision.

MISS FEECHAM: And I told you that you had no approval for this.

MRS. MANSOUR: Of course. But from my point of view, I was talking to the head of the house as a Jehovah's Witness, and I would go to the head of the house and ask. And I had a very nice visit and enjoyed my stay there on that occasion. It was quite a long visit and Mr. Freedon, I remember, after he had spoken with you on the telephone, asked if I would like to see his gun collection --

THE COURT: Mrs. Mansour --

MRS. MANSOUR: I guess I'm out of order. I'm supposed to ask questions.

At any rate, are you aware of the fact that Mr. Freedon did not ask us to leave?

MR. NUSSELL: I think I will object to that. That's also irrelevant.

THE COURT: Objection sustained.

MRS. MANSOUR: Since this is the first time I've ever tried to be a lawyer I guess I'm sort of stuck. I'd like to be put on the witness stand and have someone ask me questions.

THE COURT: If you have no further questions you will have an opportunity to testify.

MRS. MANSOUR: Very well. Were you ever aware of the fact that police were called?

MISS FEECHAM: I was aware. I was aware that police were called and that this was appropriate for the foster parents to do since you were violating their privacy. I had requested that some action be taken because this was not normal visiting and the foster home was requesting to be relieved.

MRS. MANSOUR: Were you aware that the Freedon's had come to the Ramada Inn and had dessert and coffee with me?

MISS FEECHAM : No.

MRS. MANSOUR: I suppose I have no further questions.

MR. NUSSELL: One further question. Was Mrs. Mansour given permission by you to visit the children on the 24th of March 1976 or any other time?

MISS FEECHAM: She was not.

MR. NUSSELL: I have no further questions.

MR. NUSSELL: I would like to call Miss Melanie Mansour to the stand.

Thereupon, Melanie Mansour, having been called as a witness for and on behalf of the Government, and having been first duly sworn by the Deputy Clerk, was examined and testified.

MR. NUSSELL: Please tell the Court your full name, and your relationship to Mrs. Mansour

MISS MANSOUR: Melanie Mansour. I'm her daughter.

MR. NUSSELL: Miss Mansour, let me direct your attention back to the 24th and 25th of March 1976. Were you in the company of your mother and visiting the Freedon home in Manassas, Virginia?

MISS MANSOUR: We did go out once.

MR. NUSSELL: Can you tell me whether or not you and your mother visited the neighbors in the neighborhood?

MISS MANSOUR: Yes, we did

MR. NUSSELL: Did you at that time see your sisters, Maryam and Michele?

MISS MANSOUR: No, sir.

MR. NUSSELL: Were you inside the Freedon household on that occasion?

MISS MANSOUR: No, sir.

MR. NUSSELL: Miss Mansour, do you recall being in the Court on February 24, 1976 at which time Judge Haywood entered certain orders?

MISS MANSOUR: Yes.

MR. NUSSELL: Do you recall, Miss Mansour, that the Court entered an order on that occasion that there should be no visitation whatsoever between Mrs. Mansour and the four children for a period of 30 days.

MISS MANSOUR: Yes, I recall. But it was confusing and vague, and we were never handed any written copy for a great length of time, until we finally forced it. We finally pushed our lawyer to get us one.

MR. NUSSELL: When did you get a written copy of the order?

MISS MANSOUR: I don't recall, but it was a long time after the order was issued

MR. NUSSELL: Was that prior to March 24th, when you and your mother were in the Freedon home?

MISS MANSOUR: I believe we did have a written copy at that time, yes.

MR. NUSSELL: I have no further questions.

MRS. MANSOUR: Have you found in dealing with this case that it has been difficult for you or your family to know precisely what to do?

MISS MANSOUR: It has always been very confusing and very difficult because we've never known specifically what was asked of us. We thought originally that we were brought in because my younger 4 brothers and sisters were not in school. And on January 16 we said we would put them back in schools. And therefore, we thought they would be returned back to my mother's care. However, fairly recently we found out that there were many other issues involved which the Court never brought before us. Actually some of the things that were bothering a lot of people was the way we lived our life. And now we—although it is not really the Court's business to know what we intend to do— we can thank the Court in one sense for having forced us into making some very definite plans. So we have tickets on a ship on April 23rd, which is Friday, and we are going to Israel. And there is really no reason why the children should not be returned right now, because we've done everything the Courts have asked us to do, really.

And regarding being in contempt of Court, we were not really trying to disobey any laws. We just wanted to get to know the Freedon's better so that we could ease the situation between my sisters and them. And we enjoyed our visit very much and they enjoyed it also.

MRS. MANSOUR: Now—the first visit to the Freedon family—the girls weren't seen at all, correct?

MISS MANSOUR: That's right. We invited the Freedon's to the Ramada Inn, where we were staying. We just wanted to tell them to tell the girls what was going on with regard to the case. That was all. We had a very pleasant visit all in all.

MRS. MANSOUR: The second visit that was made—do you recall what that concern was about the living arrangements for the girls?

MISS MANSOUR: Yes, ma'am. We did go to the foster home, and my mother was very upset because my sisters were put into a tiny little room with one small bed for both of them to sleep in. And this upset my mother very much because at home they each had their own good-sized bed. And she felt that these conditions, to put the twins into one bed together was not good for them.

MRS. MANSOUR: Now let me ask you about Maryam,-

MR. NUSSELL: Objection, Your Honor.

THE COURT: Objection sustained. The Court is not going to listen to any more discussion about what the respondents feel is best for the girls as justification for their having made visits.

ANNIE LAURIE: No further questions, then.

Thereupon the witness stepped down from the witness stand

MR. NUSSELL: Your Honor, I would urge that the Court find Mrs. Mansour is in direct violation of the Court's order of February 24 and is in contempt of the Court's order.

THE COURT: You represent today that you want to take the children to Israel. The children are under commitment of the Social Rehabilitation Administration until this Court orders otherwise. And the fact that you would go so far as to make those arrangements simply adds to the Court's belief that you do not intend to obey this Court's order.

It is therefore the Court's ruling that Annie Laurie Mansour is in contempt of the order of this Court issued on the 4th day of March 1976.

The Court will impose a sentence of 24 hours incarceration.

Annie Laurie is escorted out of the courtroom by police officers.

Yup, our mother went to jail. The following letter written by Annie Laurie to our foster father describes a bit of her experience there:

May 1, 1976

Dear Mr. Freedon,

Although I was sentenced to twenty-four hours in jail, I was kept for thirty. The first six hours I was imprisoned in what is known as the "bull-pen"—a small, hot, airless room with four narrow benches and a floor partly covered with water and urine and strewn with bread, cigarette butts and salami.

I was well treated in the jail to which I was finally taken, but I do not recommend the experience. I was not surprised at the conditions therein, for I was only reminded of the city schools.

My "crime" was that I had seen my children without the permission of a social worker, Mrs. Feecham.

Feeling the way you do about our judicial system, it seems that it might be wise for you and your wife to begin to consider severing your relationship with the courts as represented by the social worker Mrs. Feecham.

Sincerely yours,

Annie Laurie Mansour

Always gregarious, our mother met Carolyn Sill while in jail. Carolyn was a young black woman who had had some trouble in her life but was trying to get herself back on the right path. She and our mother formed a bond that lasted until our mother's death, with ultimately hundreds of letters going back and forth between them. Here is the first letter our mother received from Carolyn, after they had met in jail.

4/26/76

Dear Annie Laurie,

Praises in the name of Jehovah. Received your lovely card today and was exceptionally glad to hear from you. I showed all the girls on the hall your card and they all said how pretty it was. Then that wasn't enough for me I told almost everyone in 1010 how sweet it was of you to send it back. Like I told you when I met you I have no people here and it really meant a lot to me hearing from you. Tell Melanie hello and give all your other children my love. Even though I didn't get a chance to meet them all we're all spiritual sisters and brothers. I was just one of the lost sheep that strayed away from the flock. But as Jehovah says, seek and ye shall find. Which I've found to be very true. Please pray for me and my family and all of us here. I'll never forget you. We often laugh about the night you were dancing. Hopefully you'll keep writing me. Keep up the good work.

Sincerely,

Carolyn Sill

CHAPTER 13

LIBERTY

With Israel off the table for the moment, and with no hearing scheduled in the near future, we eventually got into a routine of sorts in our foster home, though yearning for a return to our family. However, as the weeks wore on and it became clearer to us that we were not about to be released from "the system" anytime soon, we started to constantly be on the lookout for opportunities to either escape or reason with the courts, as seen in these portions of letters:

April 11, 1976

Dear Mother,

We've been thinking that as the Easter holidays are coming up—that would be a good time to kidnap us. The Friday following the Memorial [Jehovah's Witnesses celebration of the Last Supper] and the next Monday we get off. The boys get the Thursday before and the Tuesday after off too. And during the weekend the social workers are off and they'll probably get a day off for Easter. So they wouldn't find out till Monday or even Tuesday.

Love,

Maryam

May 25, 1976

Dear Mother,

I guess the main reason we called you was about going to this boarding school. Mrs. Freedon said that ever since we've been out here they've been waiting for an opening in one of the schools. They're in Maryland and Pennsylvania. But I really want to get back soon after school's out and I'm getting worried that it's going to be longer—maybe a year?!

It was really fun talking to the hotel manager Mr. Oldman and I realize what a great time you must be having. He said you're making him Jewish! Anyway, he made me feel better when he said don't worry, we'll be able to come up to New York sometime.

You know, I was thinking since summer's coming up and school is going to be out soon, why can't we come and stay with you? After all, children do go on vacations and that's what it would be like—staying in a hotel. I think I'll ask Mrs. Feecham about it. Of course she'll probably say no, but it is a good argument!

Love,

Maryam

Government-granted freedom was becoming less and less likely. What we thought were "good arguments" held absolutely no sway with government-appointed social workers. Dreading a looming future of foster care until we were eighteen and could legally leave, we decided to take matters into our own hands.

Determined not to spend the summer in foster care, we planned this escape with much more forethought than the previous ones. With some cash our mother had given us we decided to catch the bus to D.C. at the stop right near our foster home, rather than walking the first thirteen miles to Washington as we had done the first time. That should give us a good head-start before the authorities had time to figure out what was going on. The bus took us to Union Station, and from there we boarded a train to New York City, where Riley met us at the train station.

We had made it! Our exhilaration was tempered by the fear that the police would somehow track us down in New York. Truthfully, we were nervous wrecks about it. So rather than stay in the city, where the courts knew my mother was residing, all of us—our mother, Riley, Melanie, and we twins boarded a train that very afternoon and headed to Kentucky, our mother's home state. We remained on the road for about two weeks, staying in hotels and visiting friends of our mother, as well as an aunt who still lived there. After the two weeks we returned to the Iroquois Hotel in New York and found the following letter awaiting us:

June 10, 1976

Dear Mrs. Mansour:

I am writing to advise you that Maryam and Michele left their foster home on the morning of June 5, 1976 without permission and without notifying anyone of their destination. Their whereabouts are unknown to us. Notification of their disappearance has been made to the DC. and Manassas police departments and the DC. Superior Court has issued orders for their return to custody.

Please advise me immediately whether the girls are with you. Thank you very much.

Sincerely,

Mark T. Nussell, Assistant Corporation Council, DC.

Did Annie Laurie love seeing that. Let them squirm; now perhaps they would know how she felt when we were taken from her and she had no idea where we were placed. She most certainly did *not* notify Mr. Nussell of our whereabouts. Years later we learned that in this type of case we apparently could not have been pursued across state lines. Though it is interesting that the D.C. courts were able to place us in foster care across state lines; that is, outside the District of Columbia.

CHAPTER 14

MOVIN' ON UP

We were thrilled to be "home," living in the Iroquois Hotel. Our mother took us all over the city, and introduced us to some of her favorite eateries: Amy's Restaurant on The Upper West Side for frozen yogurt (something we'd never heard of), Greenwich Village for falafel (again, a new-found food), mid-town for soup at Mary Elizabeth's. But it was not long before our mother realized that we needed a more permanent residence. She began scouring the papers for furnished apartments, and in doing so found a hotel offering a monthly rate. That might be perfect. If we were headed to Israel, she did not want to get locked into a long-term lease. Besides, she did not want to be bothered buying sheets and towels. We had just sold our home with all our possessions and she had no interest in acquiring things again.

Calling the number in the ad, Annie Laurie spoke to a man with an accent, someone she judged to be an older gentleman. He encouraged her to stop by and see the rooms being offered, so she and Melanie headed uptown to the Gotham Hotel at Fifth Avenue and 55th Street. Well, you could have knocked her over with a feather when a stunningly handsome twenty-seven-year-old introduced himself as Mr. Allan, the very same man to whom she had spoken on the phone. We took the rooms. (Though our mother was a flirt to the end, she never remarried nor had a romantic relationship after our father died. She certainly put her children first, though perhaps it would have been better for her and all of us had she met someone with whom she could have been a partner. She must have been lonely in later years when we had all left home).

Now, however, we were off to the Gotham (the present-day Peninsula Hotel), to live in luxury on Fifth Avenue. Our suite of rooms was on the twelfth floor, with beautiful old tile bathrooms and deep claw-footed tubs. We got to know the doormen and housekeepers on a first-name basis—it certainly helped that our mother tipped twenty-dollar-bills just about every time we entered or left the building. Bergdorf Goodman's, Bonwit Tellers, Bendel's and Bloomingdale's became our stomping grounds, not to mention Saks Fifth Avenue, Lord & Taylor, and Macy's. Then there was Central Park; we could not have asked for a grander "backyard" playground. How we loved ice-skating at Wolman Rink, then going for hot chocolate and French-fries at Nathan's afterwards. We would scoff at the tourists skating at the overpriced and undersized Rockefeller Center rink. During the summer, we would rent bicycles and ride all over the park, or go canoeing in the Central Park Lake.

A letter from our mother to Paul and Matthew's foster grandmother sheds a little light on our New York days:

July 24th, 1976

Dear Mrs. Flackmaster,

I am sorry I did not find you at home the other evening when I called, but I did have a nice chat with Donna [a foster sister of the boys]. She told me the boys were "doing fine." I certainly hope so.

It has been a long time since I have seen or talked to my boys - - - far too long. Were it not for our faith in Jehovah's purposes and the guidance He provides in the Bible, I would not have been able to withstand the pressure and the anguish. As a mother, I'm sure you can understand my feelings. We have not been idle all these months. When we contacted the American Civil Liberties Union here in New York, the head lawyer called and wrote the Washington office immediately.

They are very interested in taking this case since twenty-nine of my constitutional rights were seriously violated and it is cases such as ours that greatly concern them.

Apparently when the ACLU takes on a case, the organization leaves no stone unturned investigating every angle and it can go as far as the Supreme Court.

It is utterly ridiculous that this matter should have ever entered the courts at all. I object having to become this much involved with lawyers (even good ones), the courts (which are corrupt) and big government with its stupid bureaucracy. Since this is a very serious matter we will, through prayer, let Jehovah guide us as to what to do. He has guided us in the past—and if we continue to do His will, we are confident he will guide our steps in the future.

Mrs. Flackmaster, it was a great pleasure and a great relief to me to visit your home that one time and to know my boys were being taken care of by your very nice son and daughter-in-law. Melanie and I really wished we could have come again.

I am very grateful to your daughter-in-law, Mary, for her comforting words to the boys: "don't worry—everything is going to turn out alright!"

My husband, one of the finest men who ever lived, used to say the exact words to me whenever I became upset—especially about the children. <u>How</u> <u>comforting</u> to hear those very words again!

Jehovah answered our prayers and Maryam and Michele, my twin daughters, were returned to the family—on June 5th. It was a joyous reunion.

It is fun being in New York together. The weather is beautiful—cool breezes and sunny skies. We are enrolled as a family in summer school and in our spare time we go sightseeing. The "tall ships" were most exciting and while shopping recently at Bloomingdale's we saw the Queen of England—coming down the escalator! Fortunately, New York is a great town for pedestrians—and we do a lot of walking.

Although my children should never have been removed from their home, it has always been of great interest to us the foster homes into which Jehovah allowed them to be sent.

May we wish all of you a pleasant summer and the best of health. Special greetings to Mr. Flackmaster.

Sincerely,

Annie Laurie Mansour

As Fall approached our mother, having ended her battle with "the system," decided to enroll us twins in the prestigious (and expensive) Rhodes School, conveniently situated right around the corner on 54th Street. Located in two elegant townhouses, we started ninth grade there, and typically, were good students. Though to be honest we were very relieved when we left in May just before final exams (as to why we left early, keep reading!).

Around this same time, consistent with her plans to "make Aliyah" to Israel, our mother, along with Riley and Melanie, joined the Herzl Institute. In typical Annie Laurie fashion, she could not just be a member; she got to know the president and other executives there and would always create some excuse to visit them in their offices. She and Melanie also joined the Jewish women's group Hadassah. The summer school mentioned in her letter to Mrs. Flackmaster was a Hebrew class at the Herzl Institute. We twins soon joined them and, as usual, were diligent students, learning to read, write and speak a little of the language. To encourage our desire to move to Israel, our mother would take us downtown to Greenwich Village, where we would dine in Israeli restaurants and dance in Israeli nightclubs (Disco? What disco?) In another aspect of our Jewish education, we joined the Jewish Defense League, at one point traveling on a chartered bus to Skokie, Illinois to protest a Nazi rally being held there. We never forgot the cute Israeli boys on the bus, nor the following chants:

> Hell no, we won't go
> From Hebron or Jericho!

> Two, four, six, eight
> Israel is a Jewish State!
> Three, five, seven, nine
> There's no such thing as Palestine!

Then there were Riley's lectures. Deciding that we needed to "spread the Truth," our mother rented a ballroom at the Gotham, had Riley outfitted in a custom-made suit and Brooks Brother's shoes, and took out an ad in the Jewish Press announcing "You are invited to attend a lecture on The State of Israel by F. Riley Mansour. No Admission Fee". They managed to get a turn-out of some of the older members of the Herzl Institute, those who knew Riley and our mother personally. As for ourselves, we enjoyed the new shoes and outfits we got to wear as the hostesses of the event. Two more lectures were held, these subsequent ones in the Warwick Hotel down the block.

We never questioned the life we were leading. With Annie Laurie as our mother, we had learned long ago to "go with the flow." Who doesn't live in a hotel suite on Fifth Avenue? Certainly, we felt no regrets that we had left our home in Washington, D.C. As fourteen-year-olds, we could not have asked for a better place to be raised than New York City. We had our independence and could go pretty much anywhere on our own. No need for parents to drive us—we could walk or take the subway to get wherever we needed to go. Never a bus or taxi though! Too slow or too expensive. We have often thought, looking back, that New York was perfect for us if for no other reason than that it "grew us up." New York gave us street smarts and that experience allowed us to travel anywhere in the world and feel at ease.

CHAPTER 15

FINAL ESCAPE

While we were adapting quickly to life in New York City, the fate of Paul and Matthew still weighed heavily on all of us. We all wrote them letters constantly, and they were rather good correspondents themselves, despite being only nine and eleven-years-old. Here is one from Paul:

> July 31st, 1976
> Dear Melanie,
> Donna [foster sister] was wrong about me getting fat. When I pull my stomach in and chest out, from my belly-button through to my back is only about 3 inches, with the exception of after I eat big meal I get fat but all goes down. I'm still strait and skinny. But I do eat a lot of vegetables every meal just about. I can eat as much as I want of all kind of vegetables fresh from the garden.
> Since I have been hear I haved learned to eat crabs and boy! are they good.
> I sure hope we can get back together again and soon!
> Love, Paul

And from Matthew:

August 1, 1976

Dear Mother, & Riely,

Try to get us back!! The twins got back so can't we right, right. I can't sand it anny more.

We wan't to sail our boats but I got mad and reced mine. We can't sail them enyway. There is water way back in the woods. Did you go to a real HEBrew school?

Love

Matthew

We also love this little essay Paul wrote about life in foster care, written when he was about twelve or thirteen:

#

A Description of My Foster Father

Mr. Flackmaster was a drinking redneck who said he hated "niggers". He smoked Camel cigarettes and drank Coca-Cola at breakfast, lunch, and dinner. It wouldn't even surprise me if the old man put it on his cereal. His bottom teeth were false and he never took a bath to my knowledge, just washed up at the sink. Every week he would say to his wife "Mary, I need a haircut," which reminds me to say that if he ever stopped putting cream on his hair to keep it coal black, he would be grey within a week. Any time he was out of the house somewhere doing some carpentry work, he would never ask me to bring the tool box, just send me running back and forth a hundred times to fetch this or that. His favorite expression was "God dammit to hell". Mrs. Flackmaster was a stingy middle-aged dog. She was so cheap that she would by second hand tooth brushes and toilet tissue if they were on the market. Every time she yawned her false bottom teeth would stick out sideways like a giraffe eating leaves. Her cooking, if that is what you would call it, was disgusting! To eat a piece of steak she cooked you would have to use a hacksaw and pitch fork. The scrambled eggs she made were so terrible that the only thing they were good for was handball.

#

Since we twins had escaped, a decision was made to make an attempt to rescue the boys. Our older brother Stephen, on leave from his Coast Guard assignment in California, was visiting us in New York around August. "Putting his Coast Guard career on the line," as our mother proudly retold the tale, he rented a car, and with our mother and Melanie riding along, drove to Maryland. As they neared the foster home of the boys, they realized they were not quite sure what to do. Seeing a bowling alley across the street from the foster home, they pulled in to get their bearings and use the bathroom. Since the bathroom was only available to paying customers, they decided to pay for a game and go bowling. That must have been something to watch, since Stephen was the only one among the three who had bowled before. Our mother ended up raving about the comfort of the shoes.

After this reconnaissance of sorts, they got up the gumption and all three went up to the house and knocked on the door of the foster home. Mrs. Flackmaster, the foster mother, answered the door, and they chatted briefly with her before she brought Paul and Matthew outside. Stephen was thrilled to visit with his brothers as they showed him around the property, taking him to see the vegetable garden and the watermelon patch. Since the visit itself was illegal, Stephen thought perhaps they had gone far enough in violating the law; maybe trying to escape with Paul and Matthew was going a little overboard. At least they had been able to see and talk to Paul and Matthew. But no, that was definitely not enough for Annie Laurie; before Stephen knew what was going on, she and Melanie had each grabbed one of the boys, hurriedly pushed them into the backseat of the car, jumped in themselves, and ordered Stephen: "Drive!!" He peeled away, heading down the highway, wondering at one point whether he should detour off the main road in order to avoid pursuit. But it was already too late; a siren-blaring police car roared up behind them. Stephen pulled over, silent, while our mother and Melanie attempted to argue with the cops who approached the car. To no avail; the boys were removed from the car to be returned to foster care, and the aborted rescue was at an end. No one was cited, and the three would-be rescuers drove back to New York, demoralized and empty-handed.

Another hearing regarding custody of the boys was to be held on November 22, 1976. Leaving the two of us in Riley's care in New York City, Annie Laurie and Melanie rode the train to D.C. for the hearing. Given the poor results of prior court appearances, Annie Laurie did not hold out much hope for a positive outcome this time around; she always thought she might simply have to go AWOL and leave D.C. with the boys in tow. When it became clear that this trial was heading in the same direction as all the others, she and Melanie walked out of the court building with Paul and Matthew during the lunch break. Managing to get on a train to New York City before being traced, the escape proved successful. Paul and Matthew never returned to their foster home or the D.C. penal system.

Annie Laurie sent the following Christmas card to just about everyone involved in the case. The names have been changed to protect the guilty.

A POEM

As we ran from the court-room leaving chaos behind
We caught the new subway to the end of the line
We grabbed a cab quickly, escaping the beast
Rode the rails to New York on the watch for police
Now Fergman, now Flachman, now Feecham and
Flowers
Look Flackmaster, Freedon, these "kids" our now ours!
To the lawyers and judges and the D.A. Nussell
Friends, relatives, neighbors, we bid you Farewell!

And so we were all, finally, reunited in New York. One year after it all began, it was over. Together at last.

CHAPTER 16

MOVIN' ON DOWN

And yet this is not the end of the story. Predicted (unnervingly, to us as adults) by our Uncle Victor in that letter he had written to authorities, we ended up on the streets of New York City. In true Annie Laurie fashion, however, she made it an adventure like no other. Here is what occurred.

We ran out of money. The fifty-thousand dollars in proceeds from the sale of our D.C. home was not enough to sustain our lifestyle on Fifth Avenue. We went to the bank around this time—we were always going to the bank with our mother, bankers seeming to become her friends—and, upon learning that there was only seven-thousand dollars left asked her what we were going to do. Apparently, it never occurred to her to go to work, or to suggest her children do so, until there was absolutely no alternative. She had an intense disdain for the middle-class life. Rich? Wonderful! Poor? An adventure! In-between? *Absolutely not.* She loved to quote that Scripture from Revelation when God tells a congregation "because you are lukewarm and neither hot nor cold, I am going to vomit you out of my mouth." Middle-class was Annie Laurie's idea of lukewarm.

Though a child of the depression, Annie Laurie had never felt its deprivations. In elementary school, when asked what her father did for a living, she replied "He owns the stock market." That is because, by the time she was born he was sixty, retired from his job as a Kentucky distillery executive, and filled his days by heading to town to watch the ebb and flow of the stock market. By the standards of the day at that time in Kentucky, he was a wealthy man. And she was the spoiled youngest of four children. When the market crashed in 1929 our grandfather, Thomas Sharp Riley, reportedly turned white-haired overnight. But this seems to have been the extent of the effect on his family; while his great wealth diminished, daily financial hardship did not ensue.

Thus, having never experienced poverty or even a little bit of financial hardship, she was not afraid of it. This had been a bone of contention between our parents: our father was always concerned about running out of money, while our mother never thought twice about it. We were about to experience the repercussions of her frame of mind.

Still not interested in buying furniture or sheets, our mother "downgraded" our residence from the Gotham Hotel on Fifth Avenue and 55th Street, back to the Iroquois Hotel on West 44th Street. It was at this point that we young ones began to realize the family needed money. We will let Matthew describe in his own words how he got his first job:

#

This is the legendary John Davis. The man who first hired me to work with horses. The following took place in 1976, so I was ten.

I saw this coach drive by me on Fifth Avenue pulled by two white horses and I thought it was the absolute coolest thing ever. So for the next few days I searched for it and late one night I found it on 45th Street between Fifth and Madison in front of The Cattleman restaurant. Nobody was around. I looked and waited . . . nobody. Then I realized that there was interior seating and I knocked on the door, it opened and it was pitch black inside and I swear, the brightest smile lighted up out of that interior like the cartoon Cheshire cat's. It was John Davis and he asked what I wanted. I said a job. To this day I don't know why he said yes but he took me under his wing. My job was to watch the horses when he would take a nap or go inside the restaurant. He would split his tips with me and I made five dollars that night. It was the only five dollars my family had to our name.

Now I couldn't officially work with the horses, John wasn't authorized to hire some 10 year old kid off the streets so I would hop on after he left the stables and get off before his return. I say that, but Buster McGill was no fool (he owned the stables and you have likely seen him in movies if you watched any carriage scene in any NYC movie in the 60s/70s/80s) and he likely knew what I was up to. I would end up working for Buster and Gloria and Anita for years and I loved it. So many adventures, many with this very coach.

John Davis was an amazing man, former bank robber, heroin addict (he OD'd one night in my mother's bathroom at a carriage driver party she threw, and I had to pull the needle out of his arm and we had to sneak him out of our apartment before she noticed). The kindest, strongest man ever. He was a member of the Negro Cowboy Association and I am sure I only know a portion of his life. He was already a grandfather in this photo. He had a rough life, in and out of prison all the years I knew him and we lost contact after I left the city. I loved that man, he had the biggest heart and was a total bad ass and he was my friend.

#

Matthew, at ten years old, became the family breadwinner. But while five dollars could buy us a few hard rolls with butter for dinner, it could not pay the rent. Despite our friendship with Mr. Oldman, the manager of the Iroquois, there was not much he could do if the bill was not being paid. He apologized, but after asking us many times to leave he finally had to call the police. Soon enough, a cop knocked on our hotel room door, and proceeded to escort the whole family out of the building. We were being *evicted*. While Mr. Oldman kindly allowed us to store our few bags at the hotel, we now had nowhere to turn; we just started walking.

It was late afternoon. We ended up at a downtown Manhattan park as dusk was falling. After the seven of us shared some vanilla wafers out of a box, we four youngest ones lay down on the park benches and fell asleep. We can still feel the slats of the benches as if it were yesterday.

We awakened to the voices of our mother, Riley and Melanie discussing our next step. Police officers had told them to go to The Office of Special Housing Services on West 13th Street and so we headed there, where we were given a voucher to spend the night in the Martinique, a welfare-hotel around West 33rd Street. We had two rooms, one for the women and one for the men. What a nightmare that turned out to be—cockroaches everywhere, filthy linens. We did not want to put our heads down and barely slept, if at all. It was so bad that sleeping on a park bench was preferable to staying there. One night at the Martinique was more than enough.

When we left the Martinique the next morning and were rather aimlessly walking through Greenwich Village, we ran into one of Matthew's carriage driver friends, Jessie. He had an apartment on West 10th Street and was going to be out of town for the weekend. In an unbelievably generous act, after hearing our tale of woe, he offered us his apartment while he was away. Boy did we love that place, especially after the Martinique.

After a night or two in Jessie's apartment, we went to a shelter called Everything for Everybody, not far from Jessie's building. He may have been the one to tell us about it. Wow—it was waaay over on West 13th or 14th Street in the Meatpacking District; this was certainly a side of New York we had never seen before. Heck, we didn't even know it existed. We walked by huge warehouses displaying sides of beef, waiting for delivery or pickup. Not an apartment to be seen. Could a shelter really be around here? This was no-man's land.

Finally, we came to a building that looked like what we wanted. Peeking in the dark window, we eventually got up the nerve to enter. We had found the right place—this was Everything for Everybody and yes, they could offer us food and shelter. The whole family? Boys and girls together? Yes. And that is one thing we loved about it—Everything for Everybody allowed families to stay together. Most of the government run shelters separated men and women, which we found ridiculous. We all ate dinner at the soup kitchen there, then climbed up a ladder and fell asleep in a dank loft bed, still in our clothes. After a day or two there, we knew we had to do something about our situation. Suddenly, we remembered . . .

When living at the Iroquois Hotel on West 44th Street, we had made some friends while roller-skating in Central Park and had discovered that one of the young men lived on West 44th Street, as did we. We were thrilled to realize we might be neighbors. His "home" turned out to be Under 21, a Catholic-run shelter for runaways, and he told us all about it, and how it was a refuge for children who had nowhere else to go. So now we thought, well, we're not runaways, but we *are* under twenty-one; maybe we could stay there too.

Back uptown we headed, the whole family walking and trying to find this Under 21. Finally, we located a door with a small sign indicating this was the place. We knocked and were let in. Just us younger four knocked; our mother, Riley and Melanie stayed behind since they clearly were not under twenty-one. (Law abiding to the end, in the little things, anyway). We began to explain our situation to the young man who had opened the door. Bewildered and unsure of what to do with us, he left and returned with Father Ritter, the priest running the operation. When Father Ritter heard that our mother and siblings were nearby, he went outside to meet them. It appeared as if he had been working on a construction project, perhaps painting. He was not wearing priestly garments.

Father Ritter welcomed our family, and our mother never forgot his kindness, and by extension, the hospitality of the Catholic Church. They were opening a new wing of the shelter (probably the project he had been working on) and allowed us— the whole family—to stay there as the first guests. Even the sheets were brand new; we opened the packages ourselves. Thus began our journey on the road back up and off the streets.

Everyone who stayed at Under 21 had to help in some capacity. We were put on kitchen duty—chopping peppers, making chili, setting the table, cleaning up. We became friends with many of the run-aways and staff members, maintaining friendships with some of them that continued long after our stay ended. After several weeks, as much as we were enjoying our time there, we knew we were beginning to overstay our welcome. Out of desperation, Annie Laurie applied for and eventually received Social Security and Veterans Benefits. This enabled us to look for an apartment, and through an ad in the paper we found a sublet on West 43rd Street between Ninth and Tenth Avenues. The sublet was perfect, and one thing we ended up loving about the far West Side was the sunshine that poured down the streets. Development had not yet come to Hell's Kitchen. Most of the buildings were walk-ups, built at the turn-of-the-nineteenth century, which left plenty of airspace for the sunshine we craved to pour down the streets.

CHAPTER 17

COMPROMISE

Our sublet, in a solid, red-bricked, marbled-stepped, six-story building built in 1910, was furnished in typical 1970s décor, with shag rugs, beaded curtains, and lots of avocado-green and orange. It became home for the next several months, until the tenants were due to return at the end of August. One day, after a trip across the street to the grocery, we came back to discover we had locked ourselves out of the apartment. Plopping down on the interior steps of the building, we prepared to await our mother's return. And that is when we met Frank. Seeing us sitting there with our grocery bags, looking a little forlorn, this tall, slim, energetic young man asked us what the matter was. When we explained that we were locked out, Frank offered to let us wait in his apartment down the hall. But we had already developed some New York savvy and were not about to enter a strange man's apartment. So he just waited with us and chatted until Annie Laurie returned. Frank became a dear family friend, and our mother's theater-going buddy, until the day he died, too young, at forty-seven from what we now realize was probably AIDS.

Frank was funny, kind, a live-wire, a photographer for celebrity magazines, and the man we will never forget for berating us once for not providing "segway." In a rush to get to work one afternoon, we ran into Frank while he was stoop-sitting. He wanted to talk, and we accommodated him for a while, but were anxious to get to work on time. A chatterer, Frank made it impossible for us to gracefully interrupt him; finally, we just came out with it while he was mid-sentence: "Ok, bye, we have to get to work." Shocked and indignant but also amused, he smiled and said "Girls! You have to provide some segway—you can't just leave like that!" We all laughed. We had found a friend. Rest in peace, Frank.

#

Now that we were getting Social Security and Veterans Benefits (having accepted that Armageddon might be a bit delayed) and with a generous financial gift from Stephen for a deposit—Annie Laurie always told him the family was a good "investment"—we began searching for an apartment. Since we had begun to love our Hell's Kitchen neighborhood, we wanted to find something in the area. Boy, did that turn out to be an experience. Dismal apartments with bathtubs in the kitchen, dank, windowless hallways, rooms painted garish green . . . we were becoming more and more disillusioned as our search went on. Finally, however, a new acquaintance on the block mentioned that an apartment in her building had become available. We got in touch with the landlord, Brick Management, and walked up the four flights to the fifth-floor apartment. The hallways were dark and narrow, and we did not hold out much hope. But, oh—when that door opened! It was like heaven! Bright whitewashed walls with sunshine streaming in through the window, a "tree of heaven" blowing in the breeze outside. A whole, two-room bathroom—these days the size of many bathroom shower-stalls alone, but magnificent to us then. A new oven in the spacious kitchen, and an old out-of-work fireplace that gave the room character. Two full bedrooms, plus a living room. A "huge" closet in the middle of the long, railroad apartment. And two large living-room windows overlooking West 43rd Street, with nothing blocking our view downtown. We could not wait to move in, and we did on the first of September 1977. On the day we signed the lease we slept on the floor, using our coats as beds. No Fifth Avenue hotel had brought us as much joy.

The neighbors in our building (a former tenement which probably had an outhouse when originally built) proved to be quite a motley group, embodying a small subset of that cacophony of characters that bring life to New York City. The "supers" were a middle-aged German couple, so taciturn and private they rarely even said hello. She wore her long, gray hair in two braids wrapped like a crown around her head as she cleaned the hallways, mop and bucket in hand. They had three children, and only the youngest, by at least ten years, proved to be friendly to us. Then there was the grizzled old codger on the third floor, who walked with one arm folded behind his bent-forward-at-the-waist back, index finger pointing like a trigger. We often wondered how he managed to get anywhere . . . and whether it was he who cooked that God-awful smelling fish once a week? Sometimes he'd lock himself out and ring every buzzer in the building so as to be let in, scaring the heck out of us at two in the morning, and causing us to break things as we staggered to the window to see who in the hell was disturbing us at that hour. On

the first floor lived two related Hispanic families, and we became
friends with the daughters in each. Across the hall from us was an
Irish widow who dyed her hair a Lucille Ball shade of red, and,
when "in her cups" mouthed off at Annie Laurie and the world.
The next morning she greeted us as long-lost best friends. A
friendly black family lived below us, and across from them an
older and dignified black woman who every Sunday donned an
elegant hat as she set off to church. Annie Laurie envied her
courage in wearing hats, out of fashion though they were.

While we got to know everyone in the building, and often
"hung out" with some of the children who lived there, for the
most part we tenants kept our lives separate. While that may
have been a "New York thing," we feel it was more likely a result
of physical proximity; when the only thing separating you from
your neighbor is a narrow hallway, you tend to distance yourself
in other ways so as to have even a modicum of privacy.

We adapted without a second thought.

# # #

The school year was beginning, and we made the decision to
enroll in the public high school for our neighborhood. The school
was located uptown on Amsterdam Avenue around 60th Street;
we took a bus up and registered. Well, the school was so
overcrowded that we had to sit in the hall on the floor for some
of the classes. This was ridiculous. And we had to pay bus fare for
this? Our tenth-grade year did not last long. We discussed it with
our mother, and, not surprisingly, she was fine with our decision
to leave school. It helped that we were now old enough that we
could drop out without any legal repercussions.

What we really wanted to do was work, and as soon as we
got our working papers we began to pound the pavement,

entering any store displaying a "help-wanted" sign in the window. Finally we saw that a McDonald's in the neighborhood (around 38th Street and Seventh Avenue) had job openings, so we went there one day and waited in the long line all afternoon for an application and interview. When the interviewer, learning of our nearby address, said that they did not hire locals because they did not want their friends coming in, we confidently and truthfully replied: "Oh, don't worry, we don't have any friends."

They sent us on our way and said they would call. However, we had no phone in our new apartment, and had no idea when, if ever, we would be getting one. So back every day we went, pleading to be hired. Finally, they must have gotten tired of the persistence of these two little white girls (the entire management and crew were black) and hired us. We ran home, thrilled to tell everyone that we had jobs—with uniforms and everything!

We were not the only ones searching for and finding work. Melanie, despite a complete non-interest in animals, followed Matthew into the carriage trade and became a horse-drawn buggy driver in Central Park. Unlike most of the other drivers, she decided to dress up for the part, in the summers wearing a Gypsy skirt and headscarf that she'd made herself, and donning black gaucho pants, boots, jacket and short top hat, along with a red vest, during the fall and winter months.

Riley, still interested in his Jewish studies, went to work for a Glatt Kosher deli.

It was our mother, however, who discovered what turned out to be the family's salvation: Vasilious Kakoulides, aka Bill, owner of the gyro restaurant and cigarette stand named Syntagma Square. As our mother walked by the 8th Avenue restaurant one afternoon, she noticed and was impressed by the

fact that fresh-squeezed orange juice was available. When Bill
offered her a sample glass, she gladly enjoyed it. However, as she
thanked him and went to leave, Bill asked for payment. What?
She had thought it was free. Why, he had offered it to her; she
had not asked for it. Her indignation aroused, she gave Bill a piece
of her mind. And he gave her a piece of his right back. Thus was
born a family friendship that has lasted through the years, with all
of us continuing to keep in touch with Bill, his wife Demetra, and
their four children. And not only did she come home with a new
friend, she came home with jobs. The cigarette stand was a
twenty-four-hour operation, and Bill needed people to run it.
Wow—this was perfect! For the next several years, many of us
worked there at one time or another. Paul went on to work for
Bill in several of his other businesses as well, notably a camera
shop on West 42nd Street. Bill became a father figure to Paul and
holds a very influential place in Paul's life and heart today.

###

In 1977 Manhattan, living in Hell's Kitchen and working at a
cigarette store on Eighth Avenue was quite an experience. The
neighborhood had its name for a reason. We got to know all the
local pimps and drug dealers, though none of us fell into drug use
or prostitution. That, most certainly, is a credit to Annie Laurie. It
is not as if we didn't have the opportunity; we were constantly
being offered work by the pimps buying cigarettes from us. "Pall
Mall Green," as we referred to him, dressed from head to toe in
bright Kelly-green and a smoker of Pall Mall menthols, was a
particularly memorable figure.

We also became friends with the tenant of the apartment
that we had sublet, and he offered us a job running drugs. Again,
we decided against that, though the money was tempting. A

favorite hangout day or night was Bryant Park, which was not the idyllic park you see today. It was run down, and virtually the only people there were the drug dealers, addicts, and Mansour family members who just wanted to enjoy the outdoors.

Our mother gave us incredible freedom, and we think that was one of the secrets to our staying "on the straight and narrow." We had to discipline ourselves. Had she been constantly harping on us we might have rebelled by doing exactly what she feared we would do.

It did not take long for us to develop some street smarts. A favorite line, when our distrust of someone was obvious and, offended, they would ask "What's the matter, don't you trust me?" was: "This is New York, we don't trust our own mother." It did the trick; they would laugh and leave us alone. We learned to walk with authority ("walk tall or don't walk at all," as Bruce Springsteen put it), and if it was late at night to walk near the curb so no one could surprise us coming out from behind a building. Many times, men would approach us, especially if we were walking alone, and start a conversation. We always chatted with them, acknowledging their presence and exhibiting no fear. Sometimes the topic of conversation completely befuddled us— like the time a young man approached, asked how old we were, and then began a conversation about the "age of consent." We had no idea what he was talking about. And the time a customer asked if we sold rubbers at the cigarette stand. Thinking he meant the kind that covered your shoes in the rain, we suggested the drugstore might sell them, as well as umbrellas. Bewildered, he shook his head and walked away.

Here is an adventure Matthew had during these years, in his own words.

#

That doorway on the right saved my life. Back in the late 70s and early 80's that was a rough neighborhood [12th Avenue and 48th Street]. I was a kid, probably 14 or so working the Cattleman's Coach and helping Joe and John (two of the coolest men ever [carriage drivers]). That area was also known for prostitution and as a young man dressed as a cowboy walking up the street to work, some obvious assumptions were made. Early one morning a car drove by and they hooted and hollered at me, so I flipped them off . . . Car screeches to a halt as a passenger comes half-way out the window and starts shooting. I dove into that doorway as a bullet whizzed by. John starts yelling and when the car occupants saw a possible witness they sped off. John (an ex bank-robber) was so pissed at me for not ignoring the cat calls and risking getting shot—which he said is of course what happens when you flip off a carload of gangsters. True dat.

#

Psalm 23 comes to mind: "Yea, though I walk through the valley of the shadow of death, I will fear no evil, for thou art with me. . ."

CHAPTER 18

MOVIN' ON

Gradually, as we began earning more money, the apartment got
furnished, we found a little time for leisure, and we had the
luxury of being a little choosy about our work.

Our mother ran the household and kept the family going.
She discovered a carpenter's shop around the corner on Ninth
Avenue, and the owner custom-designed furniture for us,
including a double-decker bed for Paul and Matthew and a single
for Riley, all with drawers below for clothing. Matthew
eventually got so tall (six foot five) that we had to get a piece of
plywood in order to extend the length of the top bunk. The girls
and Annie Laurie all slept in the living room. We bought four
foam mattresses which we spread out and made up at night for
sleeping, using olive-green, scratchy wool blankets from the
Army/Navy store for covers. In the morning we folded up our
sheets, stacked the foam mattresses two-by-two and end-to-end to
make a long couch, covered that with a spread, and topped it all
with pillows. (How we relished the day, after we had moved out
on our own, when we slept on a bed that did not need to be

converted to a couch by day.) There were no teenage years of sleeping until noon and hanging out in your room all day. Get up, make the couch, eat breakfast, and off to work.

Annie Laurie also shopped at an Asian home goods store she loved, and would buy things for the apartment there, including bamboo shades for the windows, and the little glass wind-chimes she loved and remembered from her childhood.

Truly, our mother's enthusiasm was infectious. She turned what could have been a depressing situation into an exciting experience. The things we were undergoing, she told us, must have been akin to what immigrants in America encountered — and wasn't it a magnificent adventure?! One year we discovered "jellies," plastic sandals that we bought on Ninth Avenue for around $2.00 a pair and wore summer after summer. Annie Laurie loved them and could not get over how such an inexpensive shoe lasted for so long.

Annie Laurie also got heavily involved in the neighborhood, meeting the neighbors (including Elaine Stellar, reportedly a former madam) and starting a West 43rd Street block association.

News

☆

The Evening Star

West 43's

Vol. 1 No. 1   July 1985

New Flower Box Arrives

Recently a large, well-made flower box, filled full of beautiful red geraniums and ivy mysteriously appeared at our front door. Tenants are concerned as how to best care for these lovely flowers. They will need to be regularly watered. We have started a water-brigade for every Saturday morning. David and Cynthia are kindly supplying the water. Please come and join us!

The Editor

President Elected

Mr. Reddrick ███████, a long time resident of 435 West 43rd Street has been unanimously selected as the first President of the 435 Tenant Association which was started in 1983. We welcome him as head of our group.

Ice Cream

A new ice cream store has opened across the street. Paradice!

If you have any news item for "The Evening Star" please send it to Apartment 5E and we will publish it in the next edition.

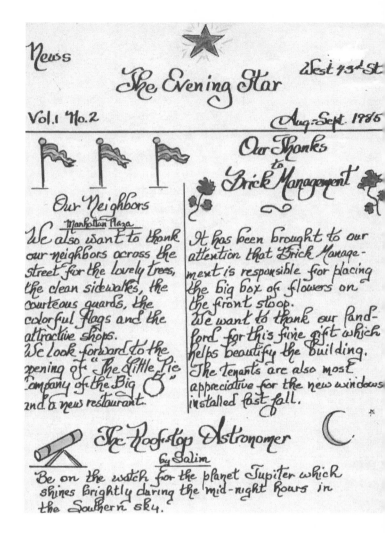

News

The Evening Star

West 43 St

Vol. 1 No. 2

Aug.-Sept. 1986

Our Neighbors

Manhattan Plaza

We also want to thank our neighbors across the street for the lovely trees, the clean sidewalks, the courteous guards, the colorful flags and the attractive shops. We look forward to the opening of "The Little Pie Company of the Big O" and a new restaurant.

Our Thanks to Brick Management

It has been brought to our attention that Brick Management is responsible for placing the big box of flowers on the front stoop. We want to thank our land-lord for this fine gift which helps beautify the building. The tenants are also most appreciative for the new windows installed last fall.

The Rooftop Astronomer

by Salim

Be on the watch for the planet Jupiter which shines brightly during the mid-night hours in the Southern sky.

She also came up with ideas for abandoned buildings, volunteered at the local public library, and just put her creative mind to work. For example, she had grand plans for the five empty townhomes next to our apartment, drawing up sketches for a club, bar, and restaurant.

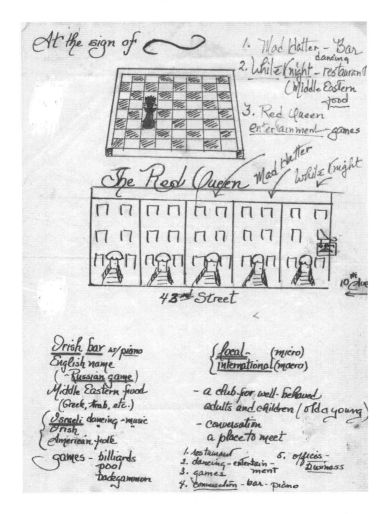

Under the overall name of 'At the sign of ~' [Infinity], and using Alice in Wonderland as a theme, it would house The Mad Hatter, an Irish bar with a piano; The White Knight, a restaurant serving Middle Eastern food; and The Red Queen, "a club for well-behaved adults and children" offering a place for games, as well as Israeli, Irish, and American-folk music and dancing. Offices would be housed in one of the buildings. Knowing her, she probably approached the property owner (our landlord Brick Management) with this proposition, but of course she had no financing to back her up. Instead, the turn-of-the-century homes were torn down, infesting us with mice during the demolition, and replaced with a bland brick apartment building.

We, as well as Paul and Matthew, all took our own laundry to the laundromat to wash, including sheets and towels. We had a big nylon sack that we would fill up, carry down the four flights of steps, place in a wheeled grocery cart, then walk around the corner to Tenth Avenue and up several blocks. We would always bring a book to read while waiting for the wash to finish. In subsequent years, when some of us went off to college, we could not get over the dependency of our classmates—you're taking your laundry home for your mother to wash? You locked yourself out of your room again? Your parents send you money?

During the summers, we would take the train and then a bus out to Jones Beach or Far Rockaway. We didn't go often, but we loved it when we did. Other times we would take our towels up to Central Park, or head up to our hot tar roof and bake in the sun; aahh—summer in the city!

Oftentimes we would just stick our head out the front window and watch the world go by; it was more entertaining than TV. Speaking of which, during the years we children lived in that apartment, we had no television. Our mother finally got one when the last of us moved out; perhaps she needed something to fill that void. (We were a little miffed at the belated appearance of a TV; wasn't that something she did not "believe" in?!)

After working at Bill's cigarette stand for some time, and then in various other jobs, we and Paul came up with an idea. What about having a fruit cart in Central Park? You could never get fruit in that area—or if you could it was an overpriced mushy apple from some deli. The Hari Krishna had fresh orange juice carts, but we wanted to have a whole-fruit cart. And there was a market for it—we were sure! Plus, it would be wonderful to have a job where we could be outside in the summer. One of Paul's job had been at a wholesale fruit market on Ninth Avenue, so we knew where to buy our stock. What we needed was the cart. After researching the prices of hot dog carts, which were completely out of our reach, our mother suggested "our" carpenter on Ninth Avenue. Perfect! We told him what we wanted: a sliding door for storage on one side, a top with short sides to hold the displays of fruit, handles for pushing, and a center hole for an umbrella. Finding a location in Brooklyn (through that now obsolete resource the Yellow Pages) that sold wheels, we took the subway out, found the warehouse, and rode back with our purchases: a pair of cartwheels for the back of the cart and a much heavier front wheel that we tried to tuck under the subway seat to keep it from rolling all over the car. We lugged those wheels up the subway steps, then rolled them down 43rd Street to the furniture store. The carpenter then attached the wheels to the cart for us. We also bought a yellow and white striped umbrella; that was our mother's idea—she loved a cheery yellow umbrella.

Finally, we were ready to go. Dressed in identical red and white sundresses and wearing our white clogs, we headed out the door with Paul early one morning. Pushing the cart up Ninth Avenue, we went into the wholesale market and bought two cases of apples, one case of oranges, one case of pears, bananas, and small boxes of raisins. Loading up the interior with our stock, we forged up Ninth Avenue then over to the entrance of Central

Park at Fifth Avenue and 59th Street. There we set up next to a falafel cart (we later got to know the owner and almost immediately began to refer to him as "Roger Falafel"), stacking the fruit artistically on the cart, and stayed there all day selling our fruit. We did not make a lot, but we did have a bit of a profit, even after spending some of the proceeds for lunch at "Roger Falafel's" cart.

Thus began our summer of selling fruit, and what an adventure it was. While we had gotten our license to peddle ($75.00!) apparently it was not always enough, and police officers often told us we had to move elsewhere. We were *indignant*—we had a license! But the police were insistent, so sometimes we sold from Sixth Avenue near Rockefeller Center, where now and then the hotdog venders would get mad because, of course, we were in their spot.

It was hard work, and we came to realize that having your own business carried a lot of responsibility. Every morning we had to decide whether to go out based on the weather—a downpour meant it was simply not worth investing in the fruit that morning. Yet no work meant no income. It was a wonderful experience, and certainly made us appreciate subsequent jobs, where, whether busy or not, we got a paycheck.

One afternoon as we were dismantling for the day an older French gentleman approached us asking to take our picture. After some hemming and hawing we finally said "ok," but when he asked for our address so as to send us a copy of the photos we replied "Absolutely not!" Hmf! Did we look like we were born yesterday? Who was this weirdo who wanted to know where we lived? With our limited language connection, we finally agreed on an address near our home, where a friend of his was living; we would pick up the photos there. In that curious way of the world there turned out to be a connection—his friend Lyse was dating a man who worked for our landlord.

We ended up developing a wonderful friendship with M. Christian Welter, who, it turned out, was a Parisian artist in New York for an exposition of his work. M. Welter loved to paint the actors and actresses of the Comedie-Francaise in Paris and sent us many a postcard copy of these works, as well as photos of his sculptures and other paintings. One year he painted a portrait of Pope John Paul II and sent it to the Vatican; it is a wonderful likeness and captures the pope's beautiful spirit. We continued to correspond over the years, and I even visited him in his Paris studio one summer and got a personal tour of the Louvre. He also offered to paint me nude. "But how could I show that to my mother?" was my initial, shocked, response. He replied that he would paint a clothed portrait too. But my conservative nature could not go for it. Annie Laurie, when I told her the story later, said "Oh, what an opportunity! You should have!"

After that summer selling fruit, we moved on to other ventures. While these days you see fruit carts everywhere in Manhattan, we feel confident that we were the first . . . in the modern era, that is!

While we were learning the ups and downs of entrepreneurship with the fruit cart, Matthew was having some working adventures of his own driving the Cattleman Restaurant stagecoach. One afternoon, while "being partners" with Dave, Dave handed Matthew an empty bottle of Jack Daniels and told him to throw it out across the street. Matthew jumped down off the stagecoach and ran across 45th Street to the trashcan there. An elegantly clad older woman saw him throw the bottle into the trash and confronted Matthew: "Did you drink that?!" Startled, he looked at her and exclaimed "No!" Not believing him she asked to smell his breath. When he inhaled to get a good breath in order to blow out the woman cut him off: "That's the oldest trick in the book—breathing in so I won't smell anything!" Matthew was shocked; he had not even realized what he was doing. The woman must have had confidence in his response. After taking a good look at him she handed him her card and suggested he stop by her office sometime. The card read "Eileen Ford, Eileen Ford Models Inc." Matthew now added "child model" to his resume. He was in numerous photo-shoots and was making by the end about five hundred dollars a day. We were astounded. He jokes now that he never saw a penny of the money he made—child slavery!

Matthew also had numerous adventures with his friends, many more than we knew of at the time and some we have just heard about recently. One that we had a hard time believing involved heading up to the roof-top of a friend's apartment building, jumping over to the roof of the Times Square movie theater next door, tying a garden hose to the billboard atop the movie theater, then rappelling down, via the garden hose, onto a fire-escape, from which they clamored down, jumped off to ground level and entered the emergency exit to the theater. All to avoid paying to go the movies.

Even at nine years old, Matthew was the family comedian. One of his favorite "routines" was walking by the X-rated movie theaters in Times Square when the family was together and asking the attendant if they offered a family discount. How we all laughed at that, especially watching the attendant's reaction.

CHAPTER 19

AFTER EFFECTS

We noted in an earlier chapter that none of the turmoil in our life seemed to upset us. And truly, we don't think it did. We were having a lot of fun—an adventure, as our mother always said. But maybe the turmoil affected us in subtler ways we did not sense at the time.

We certainly were not bored—New York City had plenty to offer, from roller skating, ice-skating and biking in Central Park, to going to movies, and of course always working. However, as things got more stable and we got a bit older, what did affect us, we think, was the lack of a vision for the future. Now what? We had an apartment, we had jobs . . . what was next? The "big picture" plan of going to Israel was not going to happen, and Armageddon did not appear imminent. We simply had no idea what to do. Our mother had always hated the notion of "boyfriends and girlfriends," and therefor none of us dated. Our role models, Riley and Melanie as the oldest boy and girl, did not even have friends. Riley studied the Bible, and had menial jobs working in delis, fruit markets, or as a foot messenger. He finally moved out on his own, but he never had any thought of "building a life," as it were.

Melanie also moved out on her own. She was twenty-six, and we twins, all of eighteen or nineteen years old, thought that was way too old to be living at home. She eventually got an apartment down the block, in the same building in which we had had a sublet. Well intentioned though we may have been, it's heartbreaking to think about now—she eating alone while we all dined together down the block. But we felt that she needed to "get a life" and perhaps we thought that would be a good start. She had some suitors among the carriage drivers she worked with but seemed to rebuff them all. Melanie was incredibly talented and could have been a clothing designer. For years, when we lived in D.C., she designed and made many of her own clothes. She had a beautiful, curvy figure, but she hated it. Whether it was because it didn't fit in with the Twiggy look of the era, it wasn't the ideal dancer's body (she loved ballet), or it wasn't the slim physique of our mother, Melanie was never happy with her looks. Because so many of the clothes in the stores either did not fit her or were not to her taste, she began creating her own. One year, after we had moved to New York, she created a seventeenth-century costume, and, taking our brother Matthew with her, entered a Renaissance fair costume-contest in Tuxedo, New York. She won first prize. Melanie was talented, driven, and persistent, all qualities which could have led to success in whatever endeavor she tried. But she simply continued to work as carriage driver in Central Park. Though she certainly did that with panache, making many of her own outfits and dressing with flair when most drivers looked rather scraggly.

Stephen had escaped to California and the Coast Guard, then enrolled in, and graduated from, The University of California at Berkley. After ten years or so, he was ready to move closer to the family and accepted a job with IBM in Poughkeepsie, NY. He had a long and successful career there.

Peter was never heard from again. We tried contacting the military, and Jehovah's Witnesses, to no avail. In subsequent years, through a connection in the FBI, we tried to track him down through the Social Security number we had for him. Again, to no avail. While most people insist he must be dead, we continue to hold out the hope of reuniting with him one day.

Paul is one of those people who was going to thrive no matter where he landed or what era he was born in. We always thought he would have been a railroad magnate had he lived in the nineteenth century. Having educated himself by reading such books as *Algebra for the Practical Man*, he applied to and was accepted by Vassar College, where he majored in economics and spent his junior year abroad at the London School of Economics. He went on to have a thriving career in the financial industry, working at Mutual of New York and Lehman Brothers before starting his own, highly successful, collateral analysis software company.

Matthew, through one of the many carriage drivers he had met in New York, was introduced to jousting. In twentieth-century America there were still people who practiced this sport. He fell in love with it, and has been jousting for thirty years, now running his own jousting group. He travels the Renaissance fair circuit throughout the country, entertaining his fans nationwide. An artist as well as equestrian, Matthew also creates beautiful leather masks and hats and sells these custom creations at Renaissance fairs and on-line.

I (Michele) found a job working at TeePee Town, a shop on 42nd Street at Fifth Avenue that sold all kinds of American Indian and western wear. I loved it, but after several years, rather down in the dumps one day after noticing the varicose veins beginning to form in my legs, I mentioned to our mother that "I'll probably be here for the rest of my life." Well, she kicked into gear to remedy this. Realizing I was floundering, she researched the Katherine Gibbs Secretarial School. Meeting me for lunch one day in Bryant Park, she showed me all the literature she had picked up and wondered whether the school appealed to me. It sure did, and before you know it, I was enrolled. That changed my life. I went on to graduate and became an executive secretary at Goldman Sachs, working with some of the top leaders of the company.

I (Maryam) had a variety of jobs, mostly retail, each for about one year. The many places I worked included the Hallmark Shop on Fifth Avenue, Mark Cross, Bank of New York on the Upper East Side, and finally, the United Nations. I was always proud of the fact that I got that U.N. job on my own. Almost everyone, when they heard I was working there, asked me "Who do you know?" presuming I had a connection in order to get the job. Truthfully, every job we got was "on our own;" the United Nations just happened to be the most prestigious and lucrative.

As for our romantic lives, well, we would meet boys while playing in Central Park but nothing that amounted to a date or relationship. Just crushes. Once we did meet two boys and arranged a date later in the week. What a disaster that turned out to be—walking around the West Side with absolutely *nothing* to say to these poor young men.

None-the-less, I (Michele) managed to meet a charming and debonair young man shortly thereafter. We eloped, moved to Brooklyn and a new life, and raised two remarkable children, William and Sarah.

I (Maryam), after working for several years, wanted a change in my life and so applied to and was accepted by the College of Charleston in Charleston, S.C., where our father had been a professor twenty-five years earlier. At twenty-years old I finally felt ready to leave home, but boy, did I feel out of place starting as a freshman. Not only was I two years older than most of my classmates, but I had been working since I was fourteen. *And* I was a "damned Yankee." It was not long, however, before I made many friends and loved how I came to understand the Southern perspective. Soon, though, I was ready to move on yet again. After two years in Charleston and following a tour of the campus of Vassar College while on a visit to see Stephen in Poughkeepsie, I decided to apply to Vassar as a transfer student. I entered as a junior the same year Paul began as a freshman.

Paul and I, as well as the rest of us, had no idea what Vassar College was, to tell the truth. Our parents were fairly negative about higher education (despite being college professors), feeling that campuses had become glorified playgrounds. Our father also felt that not everyone should go to college, that different personalities should pursue different career paths. How ahead of their time they were. We knew nothing of "Ivy League" or "Seven Sisters" and were not encouraged to pursue higher education. Yet some of us (rebels!) chose to do so. Stephen, Paul, and I ended up graduating from college, with Stephen, in his late fifties, earning a PhD in statistics from Lehigh University in Pennsylvania. After graduating from Vassar, I married and moved to Houston, TX, where I worked for an offshore-oil mapping company.

As for Melanie, she continued to work as a carriage driver, though she switched from the Irish run stables to the Italian run stables. While there, she met many wonderful people and they must have inspired her when talking about Italy. In 1981, the same year Maryam left for college and shortly after Michele had married, Melanie took all the money she had saved and booked passage on the Queen Elizabeth 2 to England, intending to ultimately end up in Italy. Soon our mother took her shopping for her travel wardrobe, making sure there would be outfits for all the on-board activities. Finally the day arrived when the whole family plus a few neighbors, including our friend Frank, walked down to the pier in the West Forties to see her off. We enjoyed a champagne toast on the dock before watching Melanie board the ship. She waved to us from the deck, where we could just distinguish her from the crowd in her new yellow and white travel outfit. As we called out "Bon Voyage" and "Don't forget to write!" we both had an uneasy feeling that we would never hear from her. "She's not going to write us," we thought.

The ship sailed at the end of July. On Wednesday July 29th, the day of the royal wedding of Prince Charles and Lady Diana, the QE2 held a celebratory dinner in the couple's honor. All passengers received a commemorative medal as a gift. Melanie was always fascinated with the royal family (we think she would have loved to marry Prince Charles), and we wonder now was this voyage specifically planned with this date in mind. It was all extremely exciting, and we looked forward to hearing about the trip.

But by October we had had no word from Melanie. Oh, how indignant we were: "well, at *least* she could have written a letter!" Annie Laurie did hear from an old friend in Europe, who was to have met Melanie in Paris when she arrived in France from England: Melanie never made an appearance. Finally, by the end of October, we received word from our mother, calling to say that we had to consider the possibility that Melanie had taken her own life. Oh my God, after just complaining about Melanie's lack of correspondence. It was too much to take in.

That farewell at the pier was the last time we were to see or hear from Melanie. Our premonition had proved true. Cunard Lines had finally returned Melanie's unclaimed suitcase, along with her unused debarkation pass, all the memorabilia from the trip—including that commemorative medal and an unopened bottle of champagne—and a note. We never found out what transpired that last night, despite numerous attempts at contacting Cunard, but she apparently jumped overboard on her last morning at sea. She was done waiting. Her personal Armageddon had arrived.

July 30th, 1981

6:00 A.M.

Dear Mother and family,

I have spent a delightful time on the ship, meeting many wonderful people. The crew are great fun and I believe Jehovah himself chose my dinner table companions. However, I did not realize until 4:00 this morning how Jehovah's name would be spread throughout the entire inhabited earth.

Please believe that I am not taking my own life but am offering myself as a sacrifice so that Jehovah's will may be known. Preparations for the marriage of his son have been made and the world has not paid any attention. The time is quickly going and "I must be about my father's business." Remember, it is a "far, far better thing I do than I have ever done. It is a far, far, better place that I go to than I have ever been."

Most Sincerely,

Melanie

P.S. Please do not cry for me for I will be with the one who will fulfill all my dreams.

Two months after finding Melanie's note, the following letter was sent to our mother from an executive of the Theodor Herzl Institute, where she, Riley and Melanie had been members:

December 2, 1981

Dear Mrs. Mansour,

I received the Xerox copy [that you sent to me] of Melanie's letter and am convinced like you that she did end her life. While I realize how much pain and soul searching you are presently undergoing, I cannot write you an ordinary letter of condolence. I say that because Melanie's letter is filled with such ecstasy that one cannot feel sorry for her. She obviously achieved a moment of complete happiness and that is something that very few people are privileged to experience. Of course, she acted selfishly since she did not think of her sorrowing family but at that moment, I am certain, she was beyond such earthly consideration.

What is most urgent for you at this juncture is that you understand her act as a consummate gift of love to her maker and not as a tool for punishing you and the rest of your family. If you see it in that way consolation is sure to follow. This consolation I sincerely hope and pray for you and yours.

With heartfelt sympathy,

Another remembrance of Melanie. One afternoon before she sailed, when several of us were sitting around the kitchen table discussing her upcoming trip and her plans to meet some relatives of the Italian carriage drivers in Italy, I asked "But what are you going to *do* over there?" Melanie's emphatic reply was "I know *exactly* what I'm going to do." My response: "You're not going to kill yourself, are you?" Had her competitive nature extended to this? Annie Laurie thought so, because Melanie knew two things: that our mother had contemplated suicide but was unable to go through with it, and that she felt the worst thing a parent could ever endure was the suicide of a child.

Which brings us back to how we were affected by our adventures. The sense of having no future, and essentially nothing to hope for did ultimately take its toll. There were many moments where we wanted to take our own lives. But something held us back; we always "kept on keeping on." Get up, go to work—we faced the day, no matter how we felt. But if death had come our way, we would have welcomed it. On airplanes, we hoped they would go down. Walking through Times Square at midnight our attitude dared anyone to bother us; we were itching for a fight, any fight. A constant deep flow of anger ran through us, but it rarely surfaced. We were happy and cheerful employees, and while occasionally sullen daughters, always showed respect to our mother, who commanded it. I wrote this little ditty in one of those moments of despair:

> Darn!
> I'll never take my own life
> I haven't got the guts
> The bravest form of copping out
> Is not for me—oh nuts!

We never discussed these feelings with each other at the time. It was only much later that we discovered we both wanted out.

And now on to Riley, the favored oldest son. We'd almost forgotten that in our "wealthy" days, pursuing somehow our "big picture" thinking, our mother sent Riley to Israel, where he promptly got robbed on Mt. Zion and had to be sent more money to the tune of one thousand dollars. We are not sure what he did there. When he returned to the States he continued his interest in the Bible and all things Israel. Riley not only gave lectures but also decided to write to Menachem Begin, the Prime Minister of Israel. His letter:

> Hon. Mehachem Begin
> Prime Minister's Office
> Jerusalem, Israel
>
> Dear Mr. Prime Minister,
> It is disheartening to note the dependence of Israel upon the United States. It is distressing to observe the indignities heaped upon the office of Prime Minister of Israel by the office of President of the United States. It causes anger to see the attacks in the press made against Israel in general and against your person in particular. It is apparent, Mr. Begin, that Israel is a much misunderstood nation and that you are a much misunderstood man.

In analyzing Israel's dilemma the conclusion that presents itself is that the Israeli government is in desperate need of a ministry of propaganda, the purpose of which would be to wage psychological warfare against the enemies of Israel along the principles of the Torah. The creation of such a department would be an act of psychological warfare in itself.

The effect of the establishment of a new Israeli cabinet-level ministry of propaganda would be immediate:

Firstly, it would serve notice to the Israeli people that Israel must become a theocracy like Saudi Arabia in order to counter Arab propaganda in its effect on world public opinion.

Secondly, it would serve notice to the world that the State of Israel exists by divine right and not on sufferance of the Arab states, the United States, and the United Nations.

Thirdly, it would serve notice to the Arab world that Israel considers itself an Islamic State in effect and that any Arab attacks on its sovereignty will require the Israeli government to declare a holy war, a "Jihad," in order to annihilate the unbelievers (enemies of Zionism) and thereby eliminate the danger to its security.

Fourthly, it would serve notice to the Palestinians Arabs that Israel under the terms of the Torah has the legal right to exterminate them to the last man, woman, and child.

Fifthly, it would serve notice to the United States government that by virtue of the legal position of the God of Israel in American law the State Department is compelled to support Israel's stand on maintaining its Biblical borders.

Sixthly, it would serve notice to the United Nations that by virtue of the moral position of the prophets of Israel in international law the City of Jerusalem is better suited to be its headquarters than the City of New York.

Seventhly, it would serve notice to the world that the purpose of the State of Israel is to become a world government to which all nations must yield their sovereignty in the same manner as the American states yielded theirs to the federal government of the United States. The Hebrew language would then become the language of diplomacy.

The office of the foreign minister would retain its present function, of course. It is not to undermine the foreign ministry that the office of propaganda minister is created but rather to have a semi-official agency which can lash out at Israel's enemies without the Israeli government having to be formally committed to its statements as a matter of domestic or foreign policy.

I would be happy to come to Israel to explain this idea further and/or answer letters serving the same purpose.

Very respectfully yours,

F. Riley Mansour

He received a response:

לשכת ראש הממשלה
PRIME MINISTER'S BUREAU

Jerusalem, May 31, 1978
A 820 (1-2) 1 400 - 1

Mr. F. Riley Mansour

New York, N.Y. 10036
U. S. A.

Dear Mr. Mansour,

      I wish to acknowledge with thanks
receipt of your letter of March 28, 1978,
and to advise you that its contents have been
brought to the Prime Minister's attention.

      With best wishes,

                Sincerely yours,

                Yona

            Miss Yona
            Personal Assistant
            to the Prime Minister

    P.S. Please forgive this late reply, due to the
unusually heavy load of mail the Prime Minister
has been receiving.

To encourage Riley to write a book using all his "big" ideas, our brother Stephen came up with this spoof review, which we have always loved. Unfortunately, it was not enough to inspire Riley.

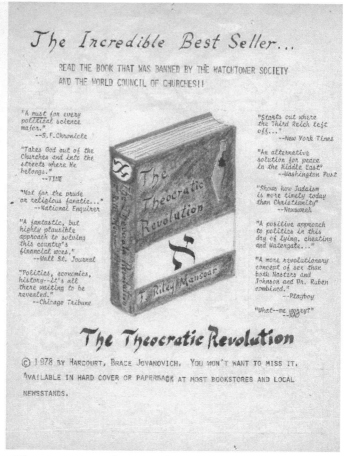

These were typical topics of conversation around our dinner table. When I went off to Vassar and heard some classmates speaking in awe about topics they were discussing in class I was a little bemused—they were nothing compared to what I had been accustomed to.

Finally, after all of this big-picture thinking came to naught, essentially becoming submerged in the realities of day-to-day living, Riley simply continued on with his life in New York: renting a room from a Greek immigrant family, working as a messenger, reading both the Bible and The New York Times daily, and attending synagogue on Saturdays.

He continues to lecture to anyone who will listen. And is still waiting for Armageddon.

POSTLUDE

New Year's Eve, 1997. Paul has bought a beautiful turn-of-the-century home in Scranton, Pennsylvania. All of us except Annie Laurie (she will join us within the year) have moved to Scranton as well, our lives elsewhere having fallen apart. Paul has most of us helping him in his new business venture; Matthew alone has followed his own path and is creating hand-made leather masks. It is a wonderful time for us as we are getting to know each other as adults. Having gone our own way for so many years, this coming together has been like a return to the Promised Land.

Paul is throwing a New Year's Eve party, and we are excitedly getting ready; this is the first black-tie affair we have ever attended. All the neighbors have been invited, our old friends from New York City will be coming, Paul has hired a live band, the event is catered . . . life is good!!

Annie Laurie arrives with Frank from New York City. Decked out in pearls, a new navy tuxedo from Saks Fifth Avenue, and her Bruno Magli sling-back heels, she enters with her usual flair, and, as always, with that bit of an edge. ("A fool and his money are soon parted" she has never tired of kidding Paul, whom she knew was anything but a fool.) As we join her, she surveys the scene with cocktail in hand and observes:

"You wouldn't be the people you are today if I hadn't made that decision to home-school."

You are so right, Annie Laurie. We thank you.

POSTSCRIPT

Annie Laurie lived in the New York apartment for twenty years, eventually moving to Scranton, Pennsylvania where, at that point, all six of us children were residing. Healthy until the end, she had walked the mile or so to downtown Scranton and back several days before she died in her bed at the age of seventy-six. Just days earlier she had emphatically stated: "I don't want to go little-by-little."

It was instantaneous, the overwhelming grief. I saw her as a person, and not simply as my mother with all the little conflicts and annoyances that entailed. She had done her best, and I could not stop sobbing.

We had become friends despite a period where I had wondered "what on earth were you thinking?" Several days before she died she looked at me and said, "It's so good to see a familiar face." How I long for the day when I will see her familiar face again.

Upon clearing out her house we found among the items in her desk some handwritten notes:

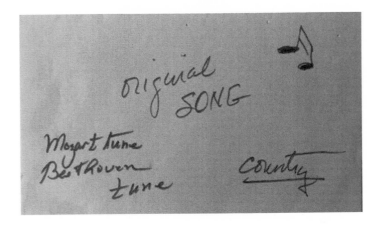

Song

He lay there a dyin' alone in the night
His life was all over no more could he fight

We called in his brother to be by his side
They sat there in silence but inside they cried

We called in his sister to bid him farewell
She leaned in and whispered some secret to tell

He lies in the graveyard, no marker- no stone
Few will remember, his name is unknown

The widow & children where now can they be?
A boy disappeared, a girl buried at sea

Life deals us a hand that has got to be played
Gambler be careful, watch how you'll be paid!

###

The following was handwritten on a piece of legal paper—she must have composed it one evening while alone in our New York City apartment.

In one box the petunias are in full blossom—the geranium has one blossom ready to burst open—in the other are a mess of impatiens and white begonia—it's November, in New York. Suddenly I tho't of my daughter. She would have loved this night - - the crisp, cool air, the dark cloudless sky, the full moon—throwing its like-no-other-light on petunias. Stranger, Melanie in the moon.

I had always been able to find the Gibson Girl in the moon, but never the man. The girl with the dark hair became my Melanie, every night always there somewhere overhead watching, waiting [for the world to awaken]

(Annie Laurie had crossed out what is in brackets)

THE END

ACKNOWLEDGEMENTS

My heartfelt thanks to my husband, Jim Axtell, whose faith and steadfastness have helped create a life for us that goes far beyond what I could have envisioned. Your encouragement throughout the writing of this book has helped me persevere to the end!

I also want to thank my son William and my daughter Sarah J. Grobeis, who have been the most amazing blessings given to me, and who continue to inspire me in all that I do, including writing this book. William, I miss our conversations and look forward to the day we meet again and I see your heartwarming smile. Sarah, your zest for life and positive outlook always cheer me up and give me a boost of energy to continue in whatever I am doing. —*Michele*

To my husband Jamie Mangan, whose love, support, and encouragement, not to mention editing, made this book possible. I could not have done it without you. —*Maryam*

To our brothers Riley, Stephen, Paul, and Matthew—we are so blessed to have you in our lives. And Stephen—a huge thanks for our book title!

To the following people who inspired us, in one way or another, as we moved forward with our story. In order of appearance as best we can remember-

When we thought it was going to be a movie:

Mark Dennebaum of TwentyfiveEight Productions. Your willingness to meet with us and enthusiasm for our story sent us soaring!

Douglas Durst, Chairman, The Durst Organization. We were so honored you remembered our family, and made the time to meet us for lunch in New York City. You were right—the story needed New York City in the original, not a sequel.

When we realized a book was more our speed:

Kay O'Brien, our first non-family reader and editor. Many of your edits remain in the book. Not only did you take the time to read and assess our story, but we could tell from your lively interest that you really liked it. Many, many thanks.

Mary Beath, daughter of our father's friend Mr. Paul Beath. We contacted you essentially out-of-the-blue, and you responded with an in-depth analysis of professional caliber. We hope the additions we made rise to your standards. A thousand thanks.

Andy Erman. You opened our eyes to the different perspectives readers would bring to the story.

Jimmy Boate, Sr. You see its potential as a musical too. (Must be the theatrical mothers we had!).

Henry Kallan, President, Library Hotel Collection. Perhaps unwittingly, you gave us the strength to forge ahead with our story.

Frank Mangan. Your thoughtful analysis gave us insight for our summary.

And to my friend Patricia Mesko. Our weekly coffee get-togethers gave me so much to look forward to while writing this book! —*Maryam*